MEET THE CONGO
and Its Neighbors

MEET THE WORLD BOOKS: MEET NORTH AFRICA
MEET SOUTH AFRICA
MEET THE CONGO
And Its Neighbors

HARPER & BROTHERS • PUBLISHERS • NEW YORK

MEET THE CONGO AND ITS NEIGHBORS

by JOHN GUNTHER

Illustrations by GRISHA

MEET THE CONGO AND ITS NEIGHBORS

Printed in the United States of America

Part of the material in this book first appeared in Inside Africa *© 1953, 1954, 1955 by John Gunther*

Library of Congress catalog card number: 59-5315

Respectfully Dedicated to
My Youthful Friend
HAMILTON FISH ARMSTRONG
in Token of Many Years of Friendship

CONTENTS

CONGO

AND ITS NEIGHBORS

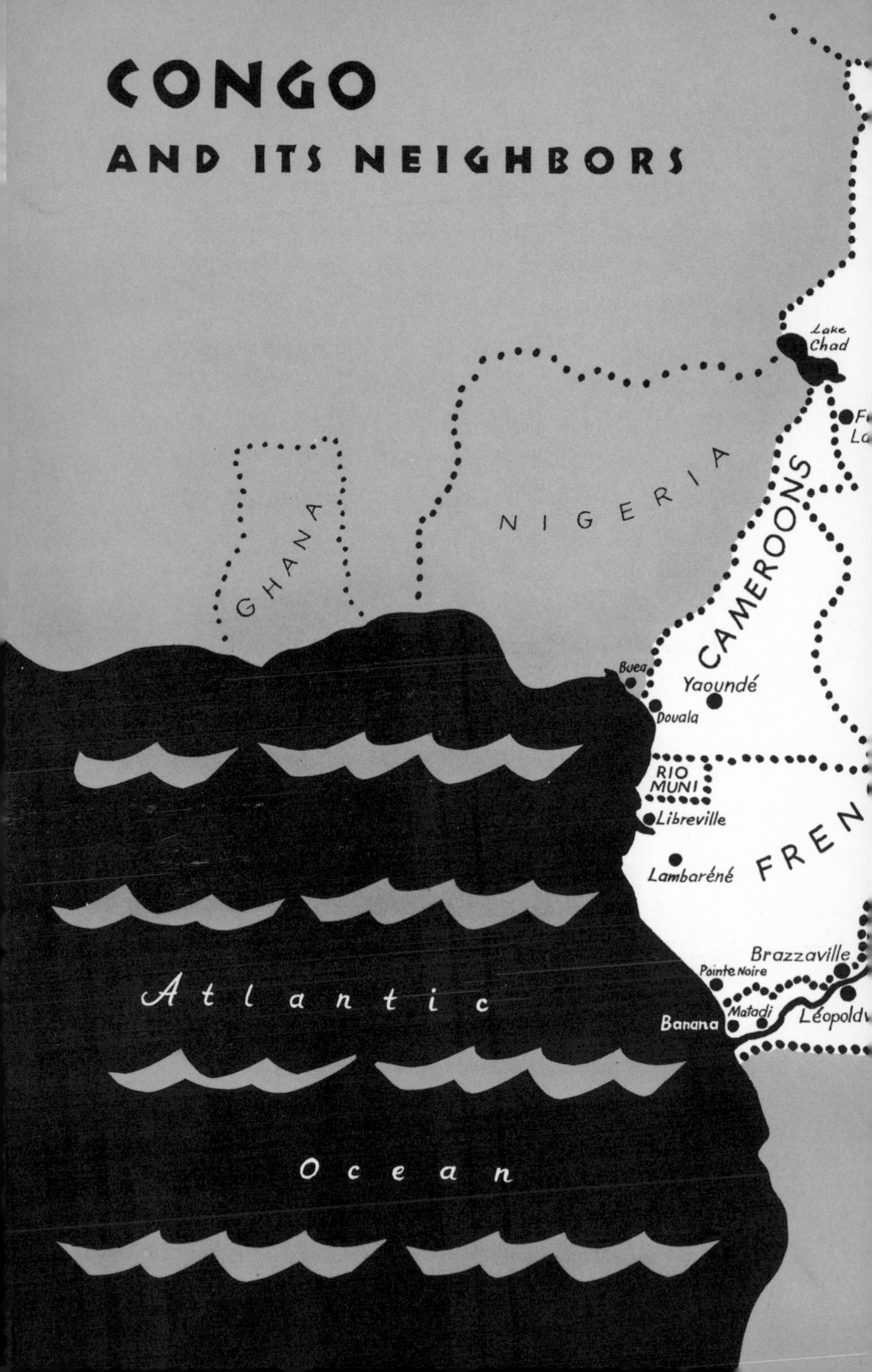

GHANA
NIGERIA
Lake Chad
CAMEROONS
Buea
Yaoundé
Douala
RIO MUNI
Libreville
Lambaréné
Brazzaville
Pointe Noire
Matadi
Banana
Atlantic
Ocean

Red Sea
Wadi Halfa
Nile
P. Sudan
SUDAN
AFRICA
Omdurman
Khartoum
Wad Medani
El Fasher
Blue Nile
White Nile
ETHIOPIA
Malakal
Wau
Juba
Bangui
Ubangi river
CONGO
congo river
UGANDA
L. Albert
Stanleyville
Kampala
Entebbe
Coquilhatville
Stanley Falls
L. Edward
Boende
lake Victoria
KENYA
L. Kivu
RUANDA
URUNDI
Nairobi
Kindu
Bukavu
Usumbura
Mwanza
Kilimanjaro
Mombasa
Arusha
Moshi
Kasai
Lualaba
Ujiji
Tabora
Tanga
TANGANYIKA
Kabalo
Albertville
Zanzibar
Dar es Salaam
Tanganyika
Elisabethville
L. Nyasa

MEET THE CONGO
and Its Neighbors

MARVELS OF THE CONGO

The Congo and its neighbors are the most exciting part of Africa. Here is the core of the great African continent, with all its majesty, mystery, and commanding romantic appeal. This is Africa at its most exotic—containing giants, Pygmies, wonderfully luxurious vegetation, unusual birds and animals, mineral wealth in great abundance, and a profusion of fascinating peoples, both white and black.

Recently I visited the Congo and the countries on its borders. First I want to describe the Congo itself, with its lively medley of problems and peoples. Then we will progress east of the Congo to the small territory named Ruanda-Urundi, a country unique in the world in several respects. After that we will go to Uganda and Tanganyika, the British territories in East Africa which are on the flank of the Congo.

Next we jump to the northwestern frontier of the Congo and look at the spectacularly colorful and varied region known as French Equatorial Africa. Here lives the celebrated missionary Dr. Albert Schweitzer, and we will visit him in his hidden forest hospital. Finally, we will inspect the Sudan, an independent country and a refreshing example of African things to come.

First, the Congo itself. Few countries in the world can match this great territory, which is a Belgian colony, for interest. Also, quite apart from elements of the picturesque and the fact that it is the heart of equatorial Africa, the Congo is an extremely important country not only to Belgium but to the rest of the world. One reason for its importance—as we shall see—is that it contains great quantities of uranium.

Few people have any idea of how enormous the Congo is. It is seventy-seven times larger than Belgium, its parent, and covers more than 900,000 square miles. If you superimpose it on a map of Europe, the Congo will stretch all the way from Paris to distant Riga on the Baltic Sea, then from Riga all the way down to Athens, and then from Athens back to

Paris. The Congo is bigger than all of western Europe, and is almost as big as the entire eastern third of the United States, that is the United States from the Mississippi to the Atlantic coast.

Until 1908 all of this immense and fabulously wealthy preserve was the exclusive property of one man, King Leopold II of Belgium. It was by far the largest and most opulent private domain ever known to history. Following various changes and reforms, it is no longer the individual private property of anybody, but belongs to the Belgian state.

The Congo lies astride the center of the African continent, and is pierced straight through by the Equator. Most of it is a low plateau, and only about half the total area is forest. Curiously enough the Congo, famous for its jungles, does not have as much jungle as several other African countries. Nevertheless it contains a wonderful variety of strange tropical beasts, like the okapi. The okapi, a cross between an antelope and giraffe, is one of the hardest mammals in the world to find and catch. Also the Congo has an animal camp where African elephants—hitherto thought to be untameable—are being trained. (The elephants you see in a circus are Indian, not African.) As to other forms of animal life, no fewer than 45,000 different species of birds and insects have been identified in the Congo—quite a number!

Another curiosity is that, although the Congo is one of the biggest countries in the world, it has only twenty-five miles of coastline—the button of territory holding it to the Atlantic.

In some ways the Congo presents a very mixed-up picture. It has large mineral resources, particularly of copper, and is a rich country in most senses of the word. For instance, it has the greatest undeveloped water-power potential of any country in the world, and it produces 70 per cent of the world's industrial diamonds. But, although potentially wealthy, it is still quite backward in several respects and many of its people are miserably poor—so poor that their circumstances of life have to be seen to be believed. In a recent year 75 per cent of the country's total income went to only 3 per cent of the population. There are some Congolese peasants who do not earn more than fifty dollars a year. The Congo has fewer than five hundred doctors of medicine for more than twelve million Africans. The first university in the history of the country was opened in Léopoldville in 1954. Since then a second university has been established at Elizabethville.

The Congo's principal source of wealth is, despite its vast mineral resources, not a mineral but a vegetable substance—palm oil. This is used locally in every imaginable way, as a lubricant, foodstuff, and source of light. It corresponds to our corn oil, and is the African equivalent of our kerosene as well. It is shipped abroad in substantial quantities every year, and is used as a raw material for soap manufacture and other purposes in England, France, Belgium, the United States, and elsewhere.

The population of the Congo is about twelve and a half million. By African standards this is a sizable figure. But by European or Asiatic standards it means that the Congo is practically empty. The density of population is only 1.8 per square mile. When Chester Bowles, the former American ambassador to India, visited the Congo in 1955, the first thing that struck him was its comparative emptiness and the fact that, as a result, it has such very large capacity for future development. The Congo is almost as big as India, and perhaps is richer, but India has more than 350 million people, as against only twelve and a half million for the Congo!

The Belgians are very proud—and justly so—of their physical accomplishments in the Congo, but in Western terms development has scarcely begun. Take railways. In the whole of the Congo there are only 3,663 miles of rail, and these are on three different gauges. Compare this to the United States, which has 389,500 miles of railway! Take roads. The Congo is an advanced country in some respects, but even today no road exists between Léopoldville, the capital, and Stanleyville, the third most important town in the country. This is almost as if no road existed between New York and Pittsburgh. Incidentally the Belgians hate to have things like this mentioned. They are almost morbidly sensitive about the Congo, and wince in embarrassment when somebody points out that it is still almost impossible to cross the country by road or rail, either from north to south or east to west.

The people of the Congo present a bewilderingly rich and brilliant variety. There are some two hundred different tribes in all. Most of these are "Bantus" —black or brown Africans who closely resemble Negroes, but who from a strict ethnological point of view are not true Negroes. Many, however, have intermarried and intermixed with Negroes for generations. The Bantus of the Congo speak no fewer than thirty-eight different *main* languages. We will have more to say about the Bantus later.

The tribes cover the widest conceivable arc. I saw primitive people near the Equator who are still naked savages, almost like those encountered by the European invaders when Africa was first opened up. They have scarcely advanced at all. But also I saw native Africans educated enough to operate complicated machine tools and drive locomotives. Some Congolese —particularly those near a river called the Lualaba— are still supposed to be active cannibals, but cannibalism is, of course, strictly against the law and the cannibals, if any, are careful not to get caught.

Some tribes are colorful in the extreme. The chief of one famous tribe, which was first seen by the great explorer Livingstone in the 1850's, is never allowed to put his feet on the ground from the time he is enthroned until the day of his death. To touch the earth would sully him. Even from his bed to his bath, he must be carried. One of the best-known Congo tribes is the Baluba. Their dynasty goes back at least three hundred years and they have produced works of art —masks, sculpture, and so on—of great beauty and distinction. The King of the Baluba is one of the most massively picturesque people in the world. He weighs 250 pounds and has 250 wives, one for each pound.

Africans in the Congo seem to be a bit happier than those in the surrounding countries. The Belgian system denies them much and Belgian rule is strict, but it also gives them much. The Congolese, even if they are poor, are probably better off physically than most of their fellows in French Equatorial Africa or in some of the British territories. At least they seem to have more spirit. Men smile; children are fat; women look contented. And they are not so drably, depressingly dressed as are most Africans in such countries as the Rhodesias and the Union of South Africa. They haven't got around as yet to adopting European dress and city ways. The Congolese in many areas still wear costumes gleaming and flashing with violent color; they prettify themselves by putting chalk marks or other mystic signs on their faces, and they love to wear brass ornaments and other glistening beads and bangles.

The total white population of the Congo is only 97,000. In other words, the ratio of white Europeans to black Africans is about one to 130. For every white man, there are 130 blacks. This is a familiar ratio all over Central Africa. The blacks overwhelmingly outnumber the white Europeans. This, in time, will produce serious problems in politics and government if the whites do not rule wisely. Nationalism—the desire of the blacks to make their own governments and have political freedom from the whites—has not been a major problem in the Congo until very recently, although it has captured much of the rest of Africa. But now nationalist discontent is beginning to be felt. In fact, serious riots took place in Léopoldville early in 1959. These were quickly put down, but the Belgian government learned a lesson from them. Reforms were launched, and Brussels even went so far as to announce that, in time, the Congo would be given self-rule and the eventual opportunity of deciding its own future.

Most of the total European population of the Congo (97,000) are Belgian. The whites who are not Belgian are in the main Greeks in the western half of the country, Portuguese in the east—traders for the most part. There are few Indians, which makes the Congo very different from East or South Africa, where the Indians form powerful and advanced communities.

One striking thing about the Congo is that the

Belgians do not encourage settlement there by their own white people. Belgian racial policy, which I shall discuss in detail later, is based on hard common sense. The Belgians know full well that what is most apt to cause political trouble in Africa is racial tension between blacks and whites. A leading cause of this is white settlement—that is, the presence of large groups of white landowners exploiting a poverty-stricken black population. The Belgians don't want to increase the possibility of racial conflict, and so they keep the white population down to the minimum.

It is perfectly true that white men run the country and that white men control practically all the tremendous mineral and vegetable wealth, but very few white people are permitted actually to *own* land. White officials come and go and white managers run the mines and industry, but no white man is encouraged to become a *permanent* Congo resident. In fact—a most unusual thing—no Belgians are even admitted to the country, tourists excepted, without posting of a sizable bond. This serves to keep the riffraff out. The Belgian authorities want at all costs to avoid having a large class of undisciplined whites on the land who might make trouble with the Africans and thus stimulate African nationalism further and provoke racial conflict.

What is even more startling is that white Belgians in the Congo have no political rights whatever. The whites are not permitted to form political parties as in Kenya, or trade unions as in Rhodesia. Politically speaking the Congo Belgians are colonial subjects, no more and no less, just like the black Africans. The Congo is still a colony pure and simple, though, as noted above, self-rule is promised in the future. As of today the European community in the Congo, numbering 97,000, must be the largest group of white people anywhere in the free world who are not even allowed to vote.

River Congo

Perhaps the most spectacular thing about the Congo is the Congo River, which flows for about 2,900 miles and is one of the longest rivers in the world. It is fed by several great tributaries—the Lualaba or Upper Congo, which was discovered by Livingstone, the Ubangi, and the Kasai. It is the only river in Africa that crosses the Equator twice, and it contains no fewer than four thousand islands.

The American poet Vachel Lindsay has described it well:

> Then I saw the Congo creeping through
> through the black,
> Cutting through the jungle with a golden track.*

* From "The Congo" from *Collected Poems of Vachel Lindsay*, reprinted by permission of The Macmillan Company. Copyright 1914, 1942, by The Macmillan Company.

Several times the giant Congo, stirring between its banks, swells out to a width of eight or nine miles. No single bridge crosses it in the whole distance between Stanleyville and the Atlantic, a river distance of some 1,900 miles. Bridges are rare objects almost everywhere in Africa.

The Congo basin covers more than 1,400,000 square miles, which is almost half the whole area of the United States, and when the river finally reaches the sea its rate of discharge is still 2,000,000 cubic feet a second, the third biggest of any river in the world. The Congo is, in other words, an extremely powerful river—even more powerful than that other great African river, the Nile. And it plays a role in the life of the Congo fully equal to the role played by the mighty Nile in Egypt.

The Congo and its tributaries are still—except for aviation—the basis of the country's communications. The Congo basin has more than eight thousand miles of navigable waters that are constantly traversed by wood-burning steamers chugging back and forth. Without the routes made by these soupy green waters meandering through grassy banks the Congo could not function as a modern state. The Congo is the circulatory system of the Congo.

On the other hand, the main stream of the Congo has not yet been completely harnessed, and is only

navigable for part of its length. Cataracts and impassable rapids cut it off in two different places—at Stanley Falls, near Stanleyville, and between Léopoldville and the sea. Below Léopoldville, the river drops 850 feet in 200 miles, and has 32 different cataracts. It has been necessary to build short railways at both these intersections so that travelers and goods can bypass the fierce, foaming rapids.

In fact, bad communications are the biggest Congo headache. For instance, the Congo produces a great deal of an important mineral known as titanium. This is alloyed with steel to make a heat-resistant metal used in jet airplanes. But to get titanium from the Congo mines to New York is a terrific task. There are at least nine different stages to the journey:

(1) Truck to Usumbura
(2) Boat down Lake Tanganyika to Albertville
(3) Train to Kabalo
(4) Train or boat up the Lualaba to Kindu
(5) Boat to Ponthierville
(6) Train to Stanleyville
(7) Boat along the main Congo to Léopoldville
(8) Train to Matadi
(9) Boat to New York or Europe

The extraordinary thing is that communications, despite all this, are as efficient as they are. As an example, large trucks carrying cotton and vegetables start out from points in the northeastern Congo and drive nonstop to Stanleyville. Here perishable goods are shipped by refrigerated boat to Léopoldville and are on the consumer's table in about ten days—not bad time at all considering the difficulties involved.

My wife and I had a wonderful day's flight along the Upper Congo. We made six or seven stops. The pilot did not always know what his next stop was going to be, because this was determined at the last moment by what cargo he had to pick up.

This was one of the roughest—and also one of the most exhilarating—flights I ever had. The first airstrip we touched on, Kindu, looked like a deserted tennis court; the airport office consisted of nothing but a grass hut with a portable telephone. Yet Kindu is an important city—both a railhead and a steamer port. At another stop, Kongola, we saw a black boy with filed teeth lounging next to a brand-new Chevrolet. Africa is a continent full of sharp contrasts.

For a while the river looked like a lion's tail; it was a clear tawny yellow and so sharply transparent that we could see the shadow of palms in the water, cut out as if by a dagger. Then the river broadened out, fed by greasy streams which soak out over the land and take the shape of clover-leaf intersections on a big American highway. In fact, the river looked almost like an automobile parkway itself, with long narrow islands in the middle resembling the grass strips that separate lanes of motor traffic.

We flew at palm-top level most of the time. The Congo is an ideal place for bush flying. Even in the sizable towns, like Costermansville, the single airstrip lies directly across from the place where passengers wait. You can see the great ships lift themselves up and tuck their wheels in from a distance of thirty feet, as they rush past like huge metal birds.

Some Congo Cities

The capital of the Belgian Congo is Léopoldville. It has been the capital since 1923. Before that the capital was Boma, down the estuary. Belgians on the spot usually call Léopoldville by the nickname "Leo," just as they call Stanleyville "Stan." The Belgians are a great people for shortening names in this way.

Léopoldville was founded by the illustrious explorer Stanley in 1881, and lies on the Congo next to a bulge in the river called Stanley Pool. (This is not to be confused with Stanley Falls at Stanleyville, which is hundreds of miles away.) Immediately below Stanley Pool the cataracts begin. They make navigation impossible between Léopoldville and the sea. But ships can sail *upstream* on the Congo from

Léopoldville all the way to Stanleyville, which is why Léopoldville was built where it is.

Directly across the Congo from Léopoldville is Brazzaville, the capital of French Equatorial Africa. The two cities are twins like Minneapolis and St. Paul. I will describe Brazzaville and its charm and character in a chapter below.

Léopoldville, a brisk little city, has about 300,000 people. Only about 16,000 are white Europeans, and if you ask the Belgians what the population of Léopoldville is, they will reply, "Sixteen thousand." In casual conversation the black Africans are not even counted, although they are a huge majority.

The present population of Léopoldville, 300,000, represents an increase from about 90,000 fifteen years ago. In other words, Léopoldville is an extremely fast-growing city. In fact it is probably the fastest-growing city in Africa. It has big warehouses stacked like packing cases along the river, broad business streets, and one skyscraper (ten stories high) which is known as "Le Building." The atmosphere is European, but Léopoldville gives an altogether different impression from other European cities in Africa, such as Salisbury in Southern Rhodesia or Nairobi in Kenya. It reflects strongly the Belgian national character. People are hardheaded, hard-working, frugal, and successful. There is no nonsense about prettiness. Léopoldville puts forth a stout note of practicality, big business, and common sense.

Léopoldville consists of two cities, one European and the other African, with comparatively little contact between them. Africans are not allowed to enter the European city after 9 P.M. except with a special pass, nor—very important—are Europeans allowed to enter the African city. The African quarter is well built, and looks much better than most African cities elsewhere on the continent. It does not remotely resemble the dreadful slums near Cape Town or Johannesburg in the Union of South Africa. There are good housing projects in construction, and the Africans have their own movies and restaurants—not many, but some. This is a great advance, and is in acute contrast to conditions in several African countries nearby.

A sports stadium was recently completed which seats 70,000 people. The week we were in Léopoldville a Belgian football team played a mixed Congo team (that is, a team consisting partly of blacks, partly of whites) and there were 65,000 blacks in the cheering crowd, 5,000 whites. Such a sight would be absolutely impossible in cities in the Rhodesias or South Africa, where racial segregation at sports events (and in many public places) is strictly enforced. The Belgians are, out of their own self-interest, quite lenient on most aspects of color bar.

Léopoldville is sprayed by helicopters carrying DDT every night, and so mosquito nets are unnecessary. There is practically no malaria. The average temperature is around 78 degrees, which means that it is pretty hot, and people become exasperated with the humidity during the long, sweltering rainy season. The worst months are between January and May.

The cost of living is very high; it is cheaper to have a chicken flown up from Johannesburg, more than one thousand miles away, than to buy one in the local market.

Parrots in large numbers fly across the river every morning from Brazzaville, on the French side, and return to French territory at night. No one has ever figured out a reason for this curious phenomenon.

Elizabethville, at the other end of the Congo, is the chief city of the great Katanga mining district. It has about 143,000 blacks, 12,000 whites. Elizabethville was founded in 1910, and is laid out in the rectangular pattern of a modern American city. It has, a rare thing for tropical Africa, street lighting at night and, something even rarer, illuminated shop windows. The elevation is 4,000 feet, and not a drop of rain falls for six months every year. Experiments have lately taken place to create artificial rain during the long periods of drought.

Elizabethville is much richer than Léopoldville because of the mines next door; its hinterland is not a tropical swamp, like that of Léopoldville. Elizabethville conveys a note of bustle, solidity, and progress. Africans living here probably have the highest standard of living of any on the whole continent. Thousands are skilled craftsmen in the shops or mines; many own their own homes, and give the impression of being prosperous.

On the upper loop of the Congo lies Coquilhatville, the capital of Equator Province. Its total European population is about five hundred. The main street of Coquilhatville lies directly on the Equator, and here are what are considered to be the most beautiful botanical gardens in the world. Stanley founded Coquilhatville in 1883, and called it "Equator Station."

Farther east is Stanleyville itself, which has about 65,000 people; fewer than 5,000 are Europeans. Stanleyville was destroyed by Arab slave raiders in 1886, and is now the capital of what is called Oriental Province. Once it was called "Falls Station," because of Stanley Falls nearby. Nothing could be more typical of the heart of tropical Africa than Stanleyville, but it is a lively commercial city too.

The most attractive of all Congo cities, to my mind, is Costermansville on Lake Kivu. This is now called by its native name, Bukavu, as a gesture to African sentiment and because Costermansville is too big a mouthful for most people to pronounce. Its location is lovely, and the surrounding country is as beautiful as the lake region of northern Italy. In the leading hotel, one of the best in all Africa, a Negro boy aged about eight wears a scarlet uniform and a flat gold hat shaped like a tambourine. He assists in opening the elevator door and acts as a volunteer guide. One day he commanded abruptly, "Give me money." I asked him why. "Because my pay is very small," he replied. This seemed to me a good enough reason, and I gave him some.

THE BELGIAN RECORD

Now a word on history. A Portuguese explorer reached the mouth of the Congo River way back in 1482, and even at that time a native kingdom of a sort was in existence. The Portuguese could not get up the river because of the impassable rapids but they made settlements to the south in what is now Angola, and converted numerous kings of the "Kongo" to Christianity. The early Congolese, particularly those near the coast, absorbed European influences rapidly. The son of one native king studied theology in Lisbon, and was made a bishop in 1520, the first Negro bishop in history. The Congo regularly sent emissaries to the Vatican for several centuries, amazing as this may seem to us now.

In the east the Congo began to be penetrated by the Arabs in about 1820. Arab slave raiders came in from Zanzibar and through Tanganyika and played havoc with the population, killing off the men and carrying women and children into slavery. The first European explorers in the modern period also entered the Congo from the east. They were seeking the source of the Nile. Livingstone thought that the Congo tributaries, which he discovered, were part of the great Nile system.

The Belgian Congo, as we know it, was created by two men, both of them characters of the most relentless will, energy, and ambition—King Leopold II and Henry Morton Stanley, the explorer. Neither was Belgian. Leopold was the King of Belgium but he was German by birth. Stanley was a Welshman who became an American citizen and toward the end of his life became a British subject again.

Henry Stanley was not Henry Stanley's real name. His real name was John Rowlands. Few men have ever had a more colorful life. Stanley was completely self-made. He was a soldier, politician, empire-builder, and journalist, as well as one of the greatest explorers who ever lived. He was harsh, impulsive, and full of ego. He was a much more dashing and extravagant character than the worthy, plodding, selfless Livingstone.

Stanley was born in Wales in 1841, and grew up in crushing poverty. His family boarded him out for half a crown a week, and he became what was known as a "workhouse boy." He determined to flee to the United States, and worked his way across the Atlantic as a sailor. In New Orleans he was adopted by a wealthy benefactor, whose name was Stanley, and Stanley took this name as his own.

Stanley had an unusual record in the American Civil War—he fought on *both* sides. He joined the Confederate Army, and was soon captured in a battle. After imprisonment for a time in Chicago he won his release by volunteering to fight for the North. Then, after the Civil War, he served in the United States Navy and later traveled all over the American West as a member of an expedition pacifying the Red Indians.

Meantime he began to write. He was a brilliant journalist. James Gordon Bennett of the old New York *Herald* sent him to find Livingstone, who, in the course of one of his expeditions, had become lost somewhere in Equatorial Africa. Stanley duly found Livingstone after a tremendously difficult and romantic search—this was in 1871—and thereafter

Africa became his whole life. He crossed the continent from east to west and discovered the course of the Congo in an epochal journey (1874-77) that cost the lives of two-thirds of his men and took 999 days. This journey led directly to the creation of the Congo Free State and the carving up of most of the rest of Africa by the European powers.

Leopold II ascended the throne of Belgium in 1865. Belgium itself had only become a country

thirty-four years before. Leopold was a vain man, greedy and energetic. He wanted prestige; he wanted acclaim; and Belgium was not big enough for his ambition. He became fascinated by tales of Africa brought back by the first explorers, and was enterprising enough to send an agent to meet Stanley at Marseilles, when Stanley was returning to Europe after his first big expedition. Thus Leopold got ahead of the other European powers.

Leopold offered Stanley a job, which Stanley was glad to accept. It is an extraordinary fact that Leopold, who became the personal owner of the Congo, never once saw Africa or visited the Congo. He never bothered to glimpse his mammoth domain. Stanley did the job for him. Stanley returned to the Congo as Leopold's man, and spent four years there working for Leopold. He was a private empire-builder for a ruthless king.

Officially, however, Stanley was not Leopold's personal agent, but was the representative of something called the Congo International Association. Leopold was genuinely interested in African exploration and development, and he wanted to give European penetration of the Congo a legal framework. Hence the Congo International Association was formed, with several European countries represented. These countries immediately got into a series of fierce disputes about their conflicting interests in Africa, and in 1884-85 a celebrated conference met in Berlin to iron them out. This marked out spheres of influence and set up boundaries in Africa which exist to this day.

The Berlin conference came to one of the most astounding decisions in history after several months of talk—it gave the Congo to Leopold outright. What was known as the Congo Free State was set up as a sovereign state under the personal suzerainty of Leopold. It was not a part of Belgium, but part of himself. And of course it was not a "Free State" at all.

Stanley's life remained full and exciting until his death in 1904. He made a third fruitful expedition to Africa in 1887-90, when he discovered the Mountains of the Moon in Uganda. Later he led a valiant —but bloodthirsty—expedition into the Sudan.

Leopold ruled Stanley's original creation, the Congo Free State, singlehanded from 1885 to 1908, when it was transferred to the Belgian government and became a colony of the normal sort. Leopold died in 1909, and was succeeded by a man who became renowned the world over as Albert, King of the Belgians. When World War I broke out in Europe in 1914, it was Albert who led the heroic Belgian resistance against the Germans.

But to return to Leopold. He was a merciless exploiter. Nobody can calculate nowadays how much money he made out of the Congo, but certainly he became one of the richest men in the world. As early as 1885 a decree made all "vacant land" in the Congo the property of the state, which was Leopold himself. Vacant land meant in effect any land which the white man wanted. Rubber and ivory, the two chief objects of value in the Congo at that time, became state monopolies, and the African natives were simply pushed out into the bush. The government had absolute proprietory rights over the whole country, and Leopold was the government.

But this was not all. Dreadful atrocities took place as the Belgians extended their rule in the Congo. The appetite of Leopold's men for rubber and ivory became voracious. African workers were made to fill impossible quotas, and, if they failed to bring in the required amount of rubber and ivory, they were mutilated or shot as punishment. Good authorities say that the population of the Congo was about 20,000,000 in 1900; today it is only 12,500,000, and Leopold's regime is believed to have cost between five and eight *million* lives.

Most horrible was the practice of mutilation. If an African boy did not satisfy his bosses, a hand or foot —sometimes both—was cut off. Photographs of such amputations are part of the record, and, if anybody wants to rake through such tragic old documents, may be looked at today.

Word of these ghastly atrocities began to leak out, and civilized people rose up all over the world in protest. Finally Leopold was forced by the pressure of international opinion to appoint a commission of inquiry to investigate the atrocities, and the outrages stopped. Then Leopold was forced to surrender the Free State to the Belgian nation and, instead of being his personal property, it became a colony ruled by the Belgian parliament and people.

The Belgian System

The essence of the Belgian system is to buy off African discontent by giving a certain amount of economic opportunity, good social services, and a comparatively high standard of living. A Belgian would define it somewhat differently by saying that the Africans should be given a sound economic structure before being allowed to advance politically. If you have a healthy economy, according to the Belgians, other problems will solve themselves in time.

Each European power which still possesses African colonies has a different idea or concept about colonialism. Each handles its Africans and runs its colonies and subject peoples differently.

The basis of the *British* system is to prepare Africans for eventual self-government. It may take a long, long time before self-government is achieved or granted, but in theory this is the long-range end in view. Eventually British colonies are supposed to evolve, with British guidance and help, into self-governing members of the Commonwealth. Then they will be free for all practical purposes.

French policy is quite different, being founded on the concept of assimilation—that is to make Africans in the long run Frenchmen. The British want to set their Africans free eventually, whereas the French want to make them *part of France*. Meantime, however, the French do a great deal to encourage political education and expression. Recently General de Gaulle, the President of France, actually permitted the French territories to vote as to whether they wanted independence from France or not. One country, Guinea, voted to break away. The others chose to remain within the French system, and are advancing rapidly to full internal autonomy.

The *Belgian* system lies somewhere between the two. The Belgians think that it is madness for the British to let Africans vote when they are still economically weak, and worse than madness for the French to work out an elaborate political structure which permits Africans to have full French citizenship and to elect deputies to Paris.

The Belgians think that they are much more realistic than either the British or the French. Perhaps they are right. Time will tell. Reform is bound to come, but the pace is slow.

The average Congolese—at the present time—has few of what we call civil rights. There is no such thing as a free press or freedom of speech and assembly. Nor are there any political rights except on a local level. The average Congolese is not, as yet, even a citizen in our sense of the term. But his children have a fair chance of getting some education, medical services, skilled or semi-skilled jobs when they grow up, fairly good pay, and above all release from the worst abuses and irritations of racial segregation, which in Africa is called "color bar."

The Congo is nothing like the Gold Coast, or Ghana, a former British colony on the West Coast of Africa, where the Africans now govern themselves. But neither is it like the Union of South Africa, where the Africans are almost totally suppressed, cruelly exploited, and submerged.

To repeat, the Congo is an example of a middle-of-the-road policy. The country is—to put it as briefly as possible—a kind of welfare state but with the people having no voice in government so far.

Everywhere in Africa the chief social and political problem is what I have just mentioned, color bar. In

America we call this Jim Crow. Conditions in Africa differ very widely on the basis of color bar. In some countries Africans are still treated almost like slaves or savages by the white rulers—for instance, in parts of Spanish or Portuguese Africa.

The Belgians, who are a humane and advanced people, like to say that color bar does not exist in the Congo, but of course this is not strictly true. Africans may be given opportunity, but they are not given equality. I have already noted that towns like Léopoldville and Elizabethville have an almost complete system of geographic segregation—they are double cities with one compartment for whites, one for blacks. And the white city is, of course, overwhelmingly favored in all respects.

There are still all manner of minor discriminations. Africans in the Congo cannot travel without a permit, they cannot possess firearms, and in theory they are not allowed to drink anything stronger than beer. They are permitted vocational education, but only up to a point. The ceiling is a curious one. A Congolese Negro can become a carpenter or a mechanic, but not an engineer. He can be a bishop, a journalist, an accountant, a medical assistant, a teacher, a civil servant, or a druggist—but not an architect or attorney. There are Negro lawyers in British and French Africa, but not one in the Congo. To the

Belgians, lawyers mean politics, and politics is one thing that the Belgians do not want their Africans to have.

One vital point of difference between the Belgian system and that of the British and French is that the Belgians do their utmost to keep their Africans out of Europe and particularly out of Belgium itself. They do not want them to see how Europeans live *in Europe*. Hundreds of African boys from British or French colonies have gone to British or French universities in Europe, such as Oxford or the Sorbonne. But practically no Congolese boys are allowed to go to a Belgian university. This is because the Belgians do not want their Africans to become tempted and dissatisfied. They feel that if Africans see what life in Europe is like they will become discontented and harder to handle politically when they return home. The Belgians do not want the Congolese to hear about things like habeas corpus, a free press, and trial by jury.

Africans in the Congo are given good social services and hospitals and so on, and are for the most part allowed to live pretty well with chances of economic advancement, but this does not mean that they are babied. We entered the Congo from Uganda and our chauffeur was a Uganda boy—a British subject. He was terrified of every Belgian we met. He had a bad cold, and we were up in the mountains in freezing rain. But he said that if we asked the hotel manager to give him a room (normally chauffeurs in Africa sleep in their cars) he would be arrested. I said that this could not possibly happen since he was a British subject, not Congolese. "Makes no matter," he replied.

I asked him if he thought that Africans in the Congo had any advantages that they did not have in British Africa. He answered, "People here have no anything."

This was an exaggeration, but certain abuses do still exist in the Belgian Congo. For instance, British officials out in the field rely largely on persuasion when they want to get something done, for example, in improving agricultural techniques or controlling erosion. But the Belgian official simply commands a peasant with some such words as, "Plant thirty trees here next month—or else!"

One complaint I heard was that if any European housewife reported that a Congolese servant had committed some misdeed, he was automatically subject to a sentence of six months in jail without a trial. Another was that boys out in the country are made to marry very young, whether they want to marry or not. The Belgians want a big, quickly expanding population. Also young men are made to work in forced labor gangs.

But we should mention again that white people

in the Congo also live under certain restrictions. The Congo whites are well behaved on the whole, and treat their Africans with respect. One word that the Africans hate is *macac*, which means monkey. In theory any white man who calls a Negro a *macac* may be fined 1,000 Belgian francs, a substantial sum. If any white man persists in abusing or affronting Africans he may be dismissed from the colony at once and, without appeal, be shipped back to Belgium.

Now a last word on segregation patterns in the Congo. There is no color bar in shops, elevators, banks, the post office, or local transport vehicles, which makes the Congo healthily different from some other African countries where such intercourse is strictly forbidden. Blacks and whites mingle freely. The Africans must be in their own localities by 9 P.M., but after that no curfew is enforced in them and they can stay up as late as they like if they remain inside the strictly African city.

In theory Africans are allowed into white hotels and restaurants anywhere in the Congo (before 9 P.M.) provided that they are correctly dressed and behave themselves. Recently in Léopoldville, Negroes were given permission to sit in the European sidewalk cafés. But comparatively few Africans care, or dare, to avail themselves of privileges like these. Many are too frightened to want to sit next to a white man in a restaurant. And the rules are not hard and fast. An American Negro representing the State Department arrived in Léopoldville not long ago. The local American consul asked the hotelkeeper if the hotel would take him in. The manager replied, "How black is he? If he isn't very dark, all right!"

I went to one big European shop in Léopoldville. It was thronged with Africans. This is a very unusual thing to see in the white man's Africa. Nothing like it could exist in Kenya, the Union, or the Rhodesias. The Belgian shopkeeper told me, "Don't think that I would be such an idiot as to have any racial segregation or color bar here! Africans outnumber Europeans by twenty-five to one in this community, and I want business. Besides in ten years or maybe twenty there won't be any Europeans left."

The healthiest thing in the Congo is the development of an African middle class. Belgians may not want Negroes at their dinner tables at home, but they do want them to have some economic opportunity. The more Africans learn skilled trades and make money, the better the Belgians like it. For the Africans to have money increases trade and makes the Congo prosperous as a whole.

And some Africans do make money. Several Negroes in Léopoldville earn as much as 20,000 dollars a year; our host's African cook had just invested

1,000 dollars in a new house. There are no fewer than 130,000 Congolese with savings accounts in the local savings banks, which is an extraordinary figure for an African country.

Finally, it was refreshing in the extreme—in contrast to the strict segregation patterns in East and South Africa—to see that Africans work in the Congo as hotel clerks, airline dispatchers, post-office employees, barmen, newspapermen, traffic cops, and so on ad infinitum. As an example, every stationmaster on the Matadi railway except one is an African. And this is as it should be.

Once on a Belgian airliner an angry white South African passenger noticed that the steward was a Negro. He was too shocked by this to say anything at all for a time, and then he burst out with a complaint, rudely calling the steward "Boy!" The steward replied politely, "Am not boy, sir. Am air hostess!"

The Congo: What Runs It

I asked Léon Petillon, the Governor General, what ran the Congo, and he replied with a quick, alert, confident "I do!" Monsieur Petillon was not being egotistical. He was telling the truth. But he was not telling the whole truth. Three things run the Congo: Belgium, which is represented by the Governor General; the Roman Catholic Church; and big business.

About each of these three factors there should be a word.

First, the Congo is as much controlled by Brussels as the island of Guam is, say, controlled by the United States. The Belgian Governor General is responsible to the minister of colonies in Belgium, who is in turn responsible to the Belgian parliament. A Belgian governor is, however, more of a free agent than a British or a French governor. In the first place he is largely independent of political pressure at home. In the second place he has no local parliament or assembly on the spot as a check on his powers, because representative government—that is the election of congressmen or deputies—does not exist as yet in the Congo.

The rule of the Belgian Governor reflects, just as does the atmosphere of Léopoldville, the national character. It is just and practical, with a delight in figures and results. Most governors are able and conscientious men, who as a rule have spent years out in the bush as junior officers, working their way up slowly and proving their capacity for administration.

All over Africa the local communities are run by men known as District Commissioners. Belgian DC's out in the hinterland keep every element of rule under their fingertips. They are apt to be sterner than French or British District Commissioners.

One interesting regulation is that a Belgian DC is not allowed to spend more than ten days a month in whatever town or village is his headquarters. During the other twenty days of each month he must keep moving—circulating from village to village and tribe to tribe. Nobody has a chance to be lazy. Also the Belgian District Commissioners are obliged to learn the local languages.

It is the Congo which makes Belgium a first-class power. Belgium is like an iceberg: the exposed fragment of motherland gets most of its weight, wealth, and substance from the huge Congo mass underneath. Therefore it is very much to the advantage of Brussels to administer the Congo as competently as possible.

Second, the Roman Catholic Church owes its tremendous power to several factors. Belgium itself is more than 90 per cent Catholic, and naturally the local administration reflects this fact. The chief immediate influence of the Catholics is on education. This is a complex story. Primary and secondary education in the Congo are not administered by the government, but by the missionaries. Incredible as it may seem, there are *no* state schools for Africans, but only mission schools or other private schools. The state does, however, give extremely important financial assistance to the missions. Of the total number of schools (26,540), 80 per cent are Catholic. Hence Catholic influence is very strong.

The first missionaries to penetrate into the Congo (in 1878) were British Protestants. Catholics began to enter in the early 1880's, but for a generation most educational work was done by the Protestants, not the Catholics. In 1925 came a measure by the Belgian government which gave the Catholic Church a monopoly on all government funds to education for twenty years. As a result state money poured in to assist the Catholic missions in a huge stream, whereas the Protestant missionaries had to support themselves and maintain their schools by private donations and their own efforts. So they were rapidly outdistanced.

No full accounting has ever been made of the billions of francs which the Catholic missions received, but the Catholics spent their money well. The Congolese educational plant—buildings, equipment, and so on—is magnificent by African standards.

In 1945 the twenty-year Catholic monopoly expired, and since that date the Protestant missions have received a share of the government's contribution to education. The fact remains that for twenty critical years, when the Congo's educational system as it exists today was being established, the Catholics had everything their own way.

The Catholics are justifiably proud of their record

in the Congo. Even in the remote bush, along the loneliest roads, a traveler will see Catholic schools, hospitals, and shrines. About 4,000,000 Congolese have been converted to Christianity, and most of these are Catholics. The Catholic Church has no fewer than twenty-six bishops in the Congo, one of whom is a Negro; there are about three hundred Negro priests.

Third, big business. This is the key to much. Nowhere else in the world, except in Communist areas where the purpose and accent are of course different, are the government and economy of a country so closely tied together as in the Congo. The Congo probably represents the highest development of what is called "state capitalism" ever attained by any country. British Africa has important commercial companies and so has French Africa. All over Africa there are ambitious development projects in which government plays a role. But the state has more authority over private business in the Congo than in any other African country. The Belgian government can dominate a corporation in a manner impossible to the British or French governments.

Five enormous holding companies—or call them trusts or economic groups—probably control 70 per cent of all Congo business. This represents a concentration of power in the hands of big business unparalleled in the modern world. Moreover in all five of these trusts, the Belgian *government* holds a substantial interest, ranging up to 50 per cent. The resulting situation is unique. The Belgian state not only derives taxes from these giant corporations but dividends as well. The Congolese cow is milked at both ends at once.

The biggest of the five great holding companies is a fabulous organization known as the Société Générale de Belgique. This was founded in 1822, and is the kind of colossus that might result if, for example, the House of Morgan, Anaconda Copper, the Mutual

Life Insurance Company, the New York Central Railroad, General Electric, and half a dozen other large American companies were all lumped together under a single management with the American *government* as a heavy partner.

The interests of the Société Générale are amazingly widespread. It is much more than a mere combination of banks and holding companies. It controls subsidiaries in cotton, sugar, drugs, automobiles, and beer. It has interests in railroads, insurance, the Belgian Aviation Company (SABENA), diamonds, cattle, warehousing, shipping, and much else.

But this is not what makes this colossus really count. What really counts is the mines. We shall talk about the mines in detail in another chapter. In passing it should be mentioned that one big division of the Société Générale is an organization known as the Union Minière du Haut Katanga, one of the foremost mining companies in the world. This company alone pays between 45 and 50 per cent of *all* Congo taxes.

Can one imagine any single corporation in any other country, even the United States, rich and successful enough to pay almost *half* that country's taxes? Then consider what enormous wealth the Union Minière must extract from the mines in order to support such a huge tax payment. A golden elephant indeed!

The Congo: Its Greatest Problems

I asked an important Belgian authority what he thought the chief problems of the Congo were, and he replied as follows: First, transport and communications. Second, harnessing of the cataracts below Léopoldville to produce electric power. Third, soil conservation.

Later I mentioned these points to the Governor General without telling him their source, and he laughed, saying, "Whoever told you that must be an economist." (He was.) Governor General Petillon went on, "The chief problem of the Congo is political education—how to get the Africans fit for future responsibility."

In this connection it is interesting to quote some remarks made by Chester Bowles, who visited the Congo recently. Mr. Bowles said, "The weakness of the Belgian program appears to be their reluctance to allow the African to secure an advanced education, for fear that he will then demand a growing share of responsibility in the shaping of his own future. The danger lies not so much in the possibility that the Belgians will not compromise eventually with the force of nationalism, but that when they do they will find the Africans almost totally inexperienced in handling the responsibilities which they are certain to demand and eventually to get."

Why cannot the Belgian system, which for all its sternness gives substantial benefits to the people, go on forever without change? Why cannot colonial rule proceed indefinitely? The reason is that, as education proceeds, the people will sooner or later be in a position to demand change. Once a certain standard of living is reached, education cannot be withheld. The Congo cannot hide forever from the modern world because it has to compete with the modern world, and this is impossible without education.

Another factor is that the people of the Congo are almost bound to be influenced sooner or later by events in the Gold Coast, which has now reached political freedom, and in such British colonies as Uganda and Tanganyika next door, where important political and social reforms are taking place. No less a personage than the Apostolic Delegate to the Congo, the representative of the Vatican, told me frankly, "Discontent is inevitable and perhaps that is a good thing, since discontent is the price of progress. The people are beginning to realize, even here, that the mines are theirs, the land is theirs."

DEEP IN THE CONGO BUSH

My wife and I had more experience of genuine back country, real tropical bush, in the Congo than anywhere else in Africa, except perhaps Nigeria. One day we went to a town called Boende, about ninety miles from Coquilhatville as the crow flies, on the Tshuapa River near the Equator. There is no road at all between Léopoldville and our destination. If we had not flown, we would have had to walk.

Then from Boende we picked up a car and drove out into the heart of the great equatorial forest. The roads are the color of rust, and they wind through

lanes of trees so heavily hung with creepers that they have the shape of parasols. They seem to be growing downward, not up. We looked at giant pink and green leaves which, to change the metaphor, seemed to form an avenue of butterflies. A scarlet and orange variety of tulip was bursting into bloom and rose as tall as a man on each side of the narrow road.

The people here are so primitive that they had no agriculture at all until the white man came; they lived on nuts and maggots, which are still a delicacy. But the Belgians are an efficient people. Some of these narrow little roads and paths, cutting across the swamps that seep down from the scummy, green river, and separated from the rest of the world as if by an enormous wet sponge and leading nowhere, are better marked than streets in such a big African city as Johannesburg.

The tribesmen we saw here belong mostly to the Bakutu tribe. They have their teeth filed sharply, and the men have extraordinary scars carved on their stomachs, scars which branch out like intricately drawn leaves; the warriors carry spears with a rattle at the tip. This means that they have given up warfare and that their spears are a symbol of peace, not of bloodshed on savage raids.

Both men and women wear a peculiar headdress—a wooden block covered with cloth which is permanently attached to their hair. Their faces are covered with red paint. Moreover the men adorn their throats with leopard teeth, and the women wear string after string—as many as thirty—of brightly colored beads. These necklaces are intermeshed so closely that, from a short distance, the beads look like a solid bit of fabric—a scarf or bib. Also the women wear scarlet beads around their loins. Otherwise they are naked.

It was very hot. On the red road two women approached, and we saw that their calves shone with gold. The gold blinked at us in the steaming sunshine. I thought that these women must be wearing boots made of some strange sparkling golden cloth. But no. What they were wearing were metal greaves of solid polished brass; these are welded to the leg from ankle to knee and weigh ten and a half pounds each. I know that this weight is accurate, because we were given one of these greaves as a souvenir and I have just weighed it on our kitchen scale.

These greaves or shackles, beautiful and repulsive at the same time, are worn by married women whose husbands are rich enough to afford them. A blacksmith fixes them on at the time of the wedding, and they are never taken off. They are called *kongas*, and are objects of great pride as well as beauty. Sometimes only the favorite wife in the family has them. We even watched women dance while wearing this remarkable African equivalent of a ball and chain. Imagine dancing with ten and a half pounds of metal on each leg!

If the husband dies the *konga* may be chiseled off by the blacksmith. But if this happens the woman will probably have to learn to walk all over again, as if she were a little child. This is because her legs have become so accustomed to the weight of the manacles that her whole body is conditioned to wearing them. When they are cut off, her leg muscles no longer have power.

Another peculiarity in this area is that many of the Bakutu carry with them a light wooden curved stool as they stroll along the roads. These stools have one leg but no arms. They are rather like the shooting sticks which English sportsmen carry. As the tribesmen saunter down the forest paths they sit down on these stools for the simplest of reasons—to rest. Apparently it is not fatiguing to carry the light stools, and it is more fun to sit on them than on the ground.

I watched native dances in several villages. The dances are somewhat placid compared to the noisy, vibrant dances of North Africa. A ring of women shuffles around a knot of drummers. The movement and music were not particularly interesting as such, but the barbaric nakedness of the bodies and the glittering ornaments worn by everybody made the performers superlatively picturesque.

These tribesmen have only one meal a day—after sundown. Men and women eat separately. Palm oil is the basis of the diet. Also manioc (the African equivalent of bread), sugar cane, and corn, are common foods. The men are expert hunters with nets, spears, and bows and arrows. They mimic closely the sounds of wild beasts, and trap them into their nets by calling them out of the trees. One favorite food is monkey flesh.

The tomtoms of these primitive folk are hollowed out of redwood trees—the same tree that makes the crimson dye on their faces. These tomtoms, or drums, can make a terrific noise.

When the villagers in this region use up a patch of soil—they wear it out after a while—they pick up their houses, which are made of portable reed slabs, and move somewhere else. They simply carry their own houses with them.

Most of the men have two wives, some three; one chief in the neighborhood has thirty. They marry as many wives as they can afford, since a woman is a useful animal. Since 1952, however, the Belgians have been trying to reduce polygamy, and by terms of a new law only the first wife in a family is considered to be legitimate. Girls marry from the age of twelve.

Wives are not only useful, but a good investment. The general rule is that a would-be groom pays a fee, known as "bride-price," to the family of the wife-to-be. The price can be as little as five dollars, and the woman then works for life.

People in this region, if they are lucky, make an annual cash income of about eighty dollars a year. Their taxes come to no more than three dollars a year. The cash crops are rice and a form of resin called copal, which is an important Congo article of export.

The infant mortality rate is very high here, as it is in most of Africa. When a Bakutu dies, he is put into one of the huge ant or termite hills that line the roads. The corpse is almost immediately devoured by millions of ants or termites. This is a simple procedure, and quite sanitary.

At a village called Wema we spent the night at a mission hospital run by the Disciples of Christ. Here Dr. Howard Horner and his wife, who are American, maintain a small hospital. Air travel and the opening up of communications, Dr. Horner told us, have brought to this part of Africa diseases never known before, like dengue fever and various forms of dysentery. So the missionary doctors have to deal not only with the traditional African scourges, like leprosy, but also maladies that have recently come from the civilized West.

We watched with intense admiration the work of the devoted American staff, under the Horners, so cheerful and courageous. What they do so admirably is done under the most difficult circumstances, thousands of miles from home and with only the scantiest of funds. Lines of sick and maimed Africans waited gratefully for treatment, as we toured the hospital grounds. One odd point is that it is impossible to teach African boys in the school softball, because they are unable to learn to catch. Nobody knows why.

Suddenly that night we walked into a funeral. A woman had been brought into the hospital too late, and died of an infection following childbirth. She was carried away in a rough brown sack, slung on a pole borne by two bearers, as a group of mourners wailed and moaned. The child, who was alive, was being cared for at the hospital by an aunt, who wore nothing but a G-string made of raffia. I lit a cigarette and tossed the match on the ground. A boy picked it up with extreme shy interest and curiosity, as if it were the first match he had ever seen. Maybe it was.

The visitor to places as utterly primitive as Boende or Wema is almost compelled to ask himself whether or not Africans—so marked is their poverty and backwardness—ever *will* be able to make progress, get ahead, and enter the modern world. But, little by little, progress does come. When the Horners arrived here twelve years ago there was not a single automobile in the whole area. Now cars are quite common. One should never minimize the basic intelligence of most Africans, or their keen eagerness to advance. They watch things carefully, and learn fast. They are fully aware of some of the white man's failings. Not without significance is the phrase for "white man" in the local language—*Lolema djola feka feka*—which means "the bat that flies hard without knowing where it is going."

The Kivu Country—also the Pygmies

Far on the other side of the Congo, in its northeast corner near the Uganda frontier, lies the Lake country. If anybody should ever be so silly as to want to visit Africa for just one week, here is where he should come. If any area on the whole continent is the "real" Africa, this is it. Here you will find anything from a Pygmy to a gorilla; the native life is overwhelmingly colorful, and the scenery magnificent beyond description.

One night at a town called Butembo, where we slept in a hotel exactly a mile high in the shadow of the Mountains of the Moon, the sunset was so rich

and rainbow-like that I thought the sky itself must be on fire. The next day, near Kisenyi, we saw the very earth on fire. Live volcanoes thrust out tongues of rosy glow over the whole gray-green landscape.

We crossed the Semliki River, which boils with crocodiles, on an ancient rickety float. Two half-naked boys poled us from one side to the other. Our chauffeur took a half-smoked cigarette out of his mouth, and gave it to one of them. This was our total payment for the passage. Then we reached the Ituri forest. This is the kind of matted jungle which the sun cannot penetrate at all.

Later we climbed a steep, shaggy escarpment and entered the Albert National Park, one of the greatest sanctuaries for game in the world. Lion, leopards, antelope, elephants, rhinoceroses, and countless other beasts roam freely on the grassy slopes. Visitors can approach these majestic animals—which are *wild* animals—in perfect comfort and safety, almost as if they are visiting a zoo, provided that they follow a few simple rules. Shooting is forbidden, and the visitor must not get out of his automobile. The animal is free, but the *man* is caged in his car.

Below we saw the flat misty plateau of the Rift Valley—four thousand feet straight down—a sea of land without end, tawny, greenish, dust-colored, with the colors merging into one another in delicate gradations and tinged by ribbons of bright haze on each side. The Rift Valley is one of the most extraordinary geological phenomena on the earth's surface. It is an immense fracture in the earth that stretches all the way from Ethiopia to Mozambique. It slices through country after country for four thousand miles, as if cut out by a bulldozer forty yards wide, and almost makes the Grand Canyon of the Colorado look like a line scratched by a toothpick.

It began to rain. This was the first time in Africa that I encountered really severe tropical rain. Rain of this kind calls its punches. You can watch a thunderstorm build up slowly, majestically, with the clouds wallowing up over the sharp spiny mountains and then making white curds in a sky still blue. The impact is as shattering as that of a waterfall. The very roof of our car shipped water. But equatorial clouds discharge their splashing cargo in the quickest of bursts; fierce, biting sunshine lights up the shimmering landscape between the showers.

The road, from Kisenyi to Astrida, is the most spectacular and dangerous I have ever traveled on. In fifty miles we saw three vehicles overturned; one was a new bright green Studebaker. It had turned over completely with its wheels sticking up helplessly in the air, like a Teddy bear lying on its back.

Until the middle 1930's this extraordinary road did not even exist. If a Belgian official wanted to go on from Astrida to Usumbura, the next important town, he had to take a bicycle or walk, and the journey took anywhere from three days to a week. The road is well surfaced now, but so full of blind turns that traffic is permitted in one direction only until twelve noon every day, and in the other direction during the afternoon. A tomtom, or a hammer banging on a tank of gasoline, gives warning of the change.

Up and down, round and round, the road climbs, circles, bobs, and twists. Round hills follow round hills, all of them green and cultivated. Never before have I seen agriculture carried on almost vertically. Every inch of the soil is used, and the intensely green fields climb the hills at angles steeper than thirty-five degrees. The basic crops are chickpeas, corn, and beans. The round huts in the villages are called rondavels, and have overhanging thatched roofs. They are scattered over the corrugated hills in a regular design so that they look like bobbins on a fisherman's net spread out by a giant.

Men along the roads wear European hats, smoke pipes, and carry spears—all at once! Children, hordes of them, surrounded us wherever we stopped, but never begged—a sharp contrast to children in most of the rest of Africa. The costumes of the women are brilliant, but the colors are not so violent as elsewhere in the Congo; they look like mottled batik, with designs that can be anything from a pigeon to a fish. The predominant colors were yellow, dark blue, dark green, and grayish violet. Almost all the women carry children—in their arms or strapped to their backs like bright papooses.

Kivu has particular enchantment. It lies at forty-five hundred feet, and, flanked by volcanoes, is one of the most beautiful lakes I have ever been lucky enough to look at. The local citizenry says that the swimming is quite safe because the water is "three degrees too cold for crocodiles." One interesting point, which shows how "new" this part of Africa is, is that Kivu, with all its beauty, was never even seen by a white man till 1893.

Farther north, between Beni and Irumu, are the Pygmies. They live in the deep forest, but it is not difficult to find them. We had no guide at all, and no white man accompanied us. We made no preparations at all. But near Beni our African chauffeur told us that Pygmies lived nearby, and asked if we would like to see them. "Yes," we said. So we bought some sugar and cigarettes as presents, drove up the road for a few miles, stopped the car, and then walked for five hundred yards or so through the dense forest.

We came to a hot saucer of rough ground, closed in by heavy branches, and here some Pygmies were. It was as simple as that.

Nobody knows for sure the origin of the Pygmies, who are certainly among the ugliest people in the world. Some authorities think that they were the original residents of Africa, and they are probably related to the Bushmen, the aborigines who inhabited South Africa in the earliest days. Many books have been written about the Congo Pygmies, and experts without number argue about their connection—if any

—with other pygmy or pygmoid people in the world, like those in the Philippines and Indonesia.

The adult male Pygmies we saw were, I should say, all under five foot tall, and some were no taller than four feet eight. They all had filed teeth, which stick out of their bright red gums like white thumbtacks—a curious sight! The Pygmies were cheerful, friendly, and as eager for our gifts as children. They proudly showed us their weapons, which included some nastily fanged arrows with teeth like a shark's. They wore nothing but a scrap of bark or liana tied around the middle, and had streaks of black—resembling coal dust smears—on their faces.

Pygmies are monogamous. It was difficult to tell the women from the men, or to know how old any of them were. One woman—she might have been fourteen or forty—had a hole drilled straight through her upper lip and in this a little bouquet of reeds projected. The children had swollen bellies, with their navels bulging out in the shape of small pears.

The Congo Pygmies are forest people who seldom see the sun, grow no crops, do no work, and live on the game that they spear or trap. Most of them are meat-eaters, but they are not cannibals. Sometimes they come into the villages and trade meat for sugar or salt. They have no villages of their own. One story told by a famous white hunter is that if a gang of

Pygmies kills an elephant, they make a hole in him and slowly eat their way out. Pygmies are as a rule despised by other Africans, partly because they are still semi-savages. A black servant will say to his master in this neighborhood, "There are four men outside, and two Pygmies."

THE BACKGROUND OF THE BANTUS

The Congo is the heart of Bantu Africa, the broad fat pendulum of territory stretching roughly from a line a few hundred miles above the Equator all the way down to the Cape. Strictly speaking this is not "Black" Africa—what the French call *Afrique Noire*. Black Africa lies mostly on the West Coast along the African bulge, and is the domain of pure Negroes rather than Bantus.

What is a Bantu?

Correctly the term is linguistic, not racial. The

Bantus are distinguished mainly by the languages they speak. There are several hundred different Bantu languages and sublanguages, but most have certain root words and other characteristics in common.

Bantus are brown, more or less, not black. Probably they came into being many thousands of years ago when two African peoples, the Hamites, who are predominantly light-skinned, and the much darker Negroes, began to intermarry. Almost all Bantus have some Negro features such as crinkly or woolly hair, flat noses, and thick lips. They are a *form* of Negro, but are not pure Negroes.

The Bantus and Negroes cover immense areas in Africa, and there are many millions of both. People wander back and forth and intermarry. So there have been widespread interweavings and overlappings between Bantus and Negroes in modern times, and this complex process still goes on. Africa is a continent in flux.

Most Bantus were originally forest people who learned to till the soil. After they cleared plots in the forest they began to raise cattle; cattle are vital to their whole way of life. Nowadays many Bantus go into the towns and become chauffeurs, mine workers, truck drivers, and so forth in the great cities, but their villages are still based on cattle culture.

The Bantu languages are quite difficult for a white

man to learn. Some, like Chinese, have special tones for pronunciation, and these can be very tricky. For instance, in one Congo language, Kele, the word *Ayeke* means both "Let him come" and "Do not let him come," depending on the pronunciation. The words for "hearsay" and "rubbish pit" are written exactly alike, but are pronounced differently. The sentence *alambaka boili* means both "He watched the riverbank" and "He boiled his mother-in-law."

Almost all Bantu tribes (and the Negro tribes in Black Africa as well) are held together by kinship. They have a strong clannishness, and are usually ruled by a chief or several chiefs.

Normally the chief is a combination of local boss, family councilor, and tax collector. He symbolizes both unity and leadership. Sometimes the chiefs are petty tyrants who are cruel to their people; most, however, are held closely in line by the white administrators above them, and strive to be well behaved. Some chiefs still deck themselves out in ostrich feathers and look like savages; they carry spears and are indistinguishable from Africans in the days of Dr. Livingstone. Some, on the contrary, are well-educated young men who wear European dress and have been thoroughly assimilated to Western ways; they act like bright junior executives in any city, drive their own cars, and talk about politics, football, and the price of beer.

Religion plays a large role in tribal affairs. Most Bantu Africans—like most good Christians—do not think that the dead are really dead. Unlike most Christians, they go further and worship their ancestors. Sometimes the local witch doctor has more influence on a tribe than its chief, because he is supposed to be closely in touch with the tribal ancestors and other spirits. One Belgian anthropologist has even gone so far as to define a tribe as "a community of the living and the dead," in which the dead are equally powerful with the living.

Spirits may take earthly form as serpents, other animals, trees, and the like, and these must be "worshiped" too.

Also phenomena like rain and lightning are supposed to be expressions of some special power in the universe that, among other things, controls the growth of crops. Hence medicine men and witch doctors do their best to be on good terms with the elements, and an unscrupulous medicine man who claims that he is responsible for bringing the rain, or stopping it if there is too much, can wield great power in the community. Almost all Africans are superstitious and anything that has to do with weather is particularly subject to superstition.

Most of the Bantus in the Congo and its neighboring states live in small round huts, which are often without windows, doors, or floors, and which are made of mud, dung, twigs, and thatch. Sometimes they have only one room, circular in shape and used by human beings and animals alike. A wood fire may burn in the room twenty-four hours a day, and those that I saw are seldom free of smoke.

The basis of the village economy is the land, plus cattle. Land is usually held in ownership by the tribe as a whole. Most people in the villages are still not only primitive, but very poor. On the other hand circumstances are gradually becoming better, particularly in villages which lie alongside the roads. The road traffic brings contact with the outside world. More and more people are able to afford soap, paraffin, cigarettes, and even bicycles. Thousands of bicycles move up and down the African trails and the grassy, muddy roads. Some of these are called "fix" bicycles because they are made out of spare parts of other bicycles too far gone to be ridden any longer.

Most Bantu Africans are seriously undernourished; the staple food is anything from bananas to mealie meal, which is ground-up corn. Almost all Africans are crazy about meat, but they don't get it very often. Hence their diet gravely lacks protein and fats. The reason why meat is so scarce is that game is not always available or easy to kill, and butcher shops are unknown except in the big towns. Most villages have no shops at all, except ramshackle stalls. Then too few Africans could afford to buy meat even if it were obtainable.

Curiously enough, the Bantus almost never eat their own cattle. Cattle are a symbol of wealth, and are too precious to kill off. They provide milk, fuel, and money for buying brides. It would shock most Africans gravely if someone should suggest that they kill and eat one of their own cows.

Cannibalism is virtually extinct in the Congo and its Bantu neighbors nowadays. But I met a British judge who had sentenced a man in Uganda to death as recently as 1937 for boiling and eating a baby. Sometimes on long trips Europeans change their African porters every fifty or sixty miles, so that the porters can return to their homes without danger of being ambushed and eaten in hostile territory. One reason for cannibalism was the widespread belief that if you killed an enemy and ate his heart or other organs, his spirit then entered your body and gave you additional strength. Another was craving for meat. A youthful human thigh was more tender and probably tasted better than a muscular haunch of antelope.

Travel for a white man is almost perfectly safe all over the huge Bantu area. In fact, the deepest thickets in the bush are probably safer for a law-abiding traveler than New York's Central Park at night. Africans have their own strict codes of behavior, and are almost always courteous to a white man. Of course, in most areas they would be afraid of being punished if they acted otherwise. Also in most parts of Bantu Africa the natives are forbidden to use or possess firearms and are not, in theory, allowed to drink hard liquor.

One curious point about Africans, with their shiny

black or dark brown skins, is that a newly born baby is not black at all, but is pink. The darkening of the skin comes later. No one really knows why Africans have dark skins. One theory is that it is a defense given by nature against the tropical sun. As a matter of fact a really jet-black Congolese is comparatively rare. They may be of any color from pale yellowish-brown to a light tan, chocolate, bronze, or a very dark gray, the color of asphalt.

The frizzy or crinkly hair of Africans is not a sign of primitiveness or backwardness, as many ignorant people believe. One authority says that the hair of the white man resembles that of the higher apes more than does the hair of Negroes. Monkeys have straight hair!

Experts on Africa differ as to how basically intelligent and educatable the Bantus are. Much scientific work has been done such as measuring their skulls and otherwise trying to estimate their potential brain power. Most Africans in the Congo regions have good memories if they are interested in a subject; most lack a sense of time. They are wonderfully good mimics. Some, undeniably, are lazy. But their laziness may result from physical apathy caused by undernourishment.

Their philosophical attitudes are very interesting. For instance, prisons were unknown in Africa before the white man came. The African attitude toward punishment was altogether different from ours. It seemed extremely silly to the Congolese that offenders against society should be cooped up in a jail and fed at the public's expense. They had other methods of punishment—some very cruel—and others not so cruel, like fines.

One reason why Africans seem to be so backward —and enormous numbers of them are undeniably backward—is that the tempo of recent developments has been so fast. Until yesterday most Africans never thought beyond such conceptions as family, clan, and tribe. Now they are compelled to think in such terms as "nation" and "world." There are certainly millions of stupid Africans, just as there are millions of stupid Russians, Americans, or what you will. But there are other millions who, if they are given opportunity, training, and confidence, will probably turn out to be just as intelligent as white men. The color of a person's skin has very little to do with his intellectual capacity. There is no scientific justification for assuming that any people are inferior or "different" purely on grounds of color.

Almost all Africans, no matter where they live or what kind of skins they have, crave education. They do not get anything like the facilities for education they deserve, and this is one reason why they may seem childish or confused. In some parts of Bantu Africa only 8 per cent of children of school age go to school, because there are so few schools.

It is frequently said that what Africa needs most is what the Congo specializes in—*vocational* education, the training that will make men bricklayers, pipe fitters, mechanics, and so on, rather than salesmen, clerks, or government officials. True. But a solid grounding in the three R's should come first. *Can* illiteracy be wiped out? Of course. The example of the Philippines proves this emphatically, and so does India.

Bantu Africans are by and large a sunny people, cheerful, gregarious, inquisitive, and, in spite of everything, fairly happy. They are much warmer, gentler, and more relaxed than people to the north like the scornful Arabs or arrogant Ethiopians. They love companionship, and take a great delight in music, art, and spectacle.

You can drive for hours along a forest road in the Congo and not see a soul between villages. Have a flat tire, and instantly, in a matter of seconds, there will be a dozen Africans appearing miraculously out of the bush from nowhere, thronging the road, watching and chortling humorously. And it is the easiest thing in the world to pick up a passenger without having the faintest idea where he came from.

Stop along a road for a moment, particularly at night, and presto! a grinning native has climbed into your car and is perched on the seat next to your chauffeur. It is very strange.

Females of the Species

Africans love to carry things on their heads, and they do so with a wonderful sense of balance. The old story is that if you give an African a wheelbarrow to help him with his burdens, he will even carry the wheelbarrow on his head.

I have seen Africans, particularly women, carry everything from bottles standing upright to a mattress on their heads while taking a walk. Small children are usually slung over the back and tied on, so that the woman has her hands free for other duties, such as clubbing a donkey with a stick. Men seldom carry anything, but walk ahead, scouting out the way; this derives from olden days when it was the duty of the male to watch out for wild animals or enemy raiders. As a matter of fact this division of labor does not differ very much from that of California or Surrey; mostly it is women who do the shopping, and transport their purchases home. I asked a District Commissioner why comparatively well-off Congolese, who could afford bicycles, did not buy carts or other mechanical contrivances for carrying their heavy loads.

His answer was, "Women are cheaper, and do not need spare parts."

Never—not even in the Andes—have I seen women carry so much or seem so much like beasts of burden as women in Bantu Africa. It isn't at all unusual for a woman to carry a load of one hundred pounds of firewood. This compares with the standard load of sixty pounds for a professional porter. A prisoner doing hard labor is not obliged to carry more than fourteen pounds.

Women play a substantial role in most Congolese communities. Maybe they look like slaves and they certainly do plenty of hard work, but they have well-defined rights and privileges as well as duties. They are not prisoners or drones like most women in Moslem areas. They expect a reward for their labors, and have certain rights to property which even their husbands cannot interfere with. On the other hand, women form a class more backward than men from the point of education. It is harder to teach them Western standards because as a rule they have never gone to school at all, and do not know any language but their own. Hence they have little opportunity to see how white people live and behave.

Marriage customs are very complex. Most tribes in Central Africa are polygamous, without limit to the number of wives a man may have. One reason for polygamy is economics. The more wives a man has the more workers are available to watch his cattle or tend his fields. Also to have a number of wives increases the possibility of having numerous children, who are also useful as workers. Another reason for polygamy lies in the realm of symbolism and superstition. Many Africans think that the ability to have many children has an association with the fertility of the soil, on which daily life depends.

Most marriages are accompanied by bride-price. This is the sum paid by a man for his wife to the bride's family. Nine times out of ten the bride-price is paid in cattle. When cattle are not available, cash, merchandise, or services may be tendered instead; the groom-to-be may hire himself out to the bride's father for work in the fields. In the Congo the normal bride-price is the equivalent of three heifers. But it should be pointed out that bride-price is more than merely a commercial transaction. It is a kind of insurance. A father's children are, together with his cattle, the "capital" of the family, on which it is only fair that he should have some return. If he loses a daughter, he should get an animal or two in exchange. The ability to pay bride-price shows that the groom is serious in his intentions, has a certain amount of wealth, and has reached a respectable status in society.

Inheritance almost everywhere in Bantu Africa is

from the mother's side, not the father's. A nephew inherits rather than a son, and the old woman of the tribe is often more important than the old man.

Witchcraft and Black Magic

Belief in magic is almost universal throughout the Congo regions, and so is fear of witchcraft. Magic and witchcraft are quite different things. In most communities there are two different types of witch doctors. One is the simple magician or medicine man who brews herbs, prescribes potions, and often has remarkable success in curing illness. He *is* a kind of doctor. But his power to heal comes not only from his medicines, but because he is supposed to have intimate contact with the tribal spirits, that is, the ancestors of members of the tribe.

The other type of witch doctor, who is called a *Boloki* in the Congo, is altogether different. He is the devil of the community, and a nasty customer. He is a sorcerer, who casts spells and is hired to do injury to others. He may even murder people—for a fee—by poison or other means. A favorite place to carry poison, if you have purchased some from a witch doctor, is under the little fingernail. You dip your finger into the cup from which the victim may be drinking, without anybody seeing it, and he is done for.

There are 570 different African plants known to

Western science that are poisonous to some degree or other. No doubt the *Bolokis* know many more.

Most anthropologists think that witchcraft gives the primitive African a sense of power against the elemental forces of nature. Man alone is not strong enough to cope with nature—tropical storms, drought, and so forth—and so he is driven to rely on the supernatural for assistance. In a way witchcraft is the African's substitute for our Almighty. In Western religions, the concept of God is the link between the human being and the mysterious forces of the universe; similarly primitive Africans believe in spirits.

Few Africans out in the bush think that anyone ever dies a "natural" death. A spell must have been put on the dead man, or he would not have died. If a man is sick, it merely means that he is bewitched. Hence Africans hire witch doctors to put spells on their enemies, in order to make them sick, or to avert spells put on themselves by others. I met one African who was a university graduate but who nevertheless told me, discussing these matters, "Yes, I know that a European doctor may be able to cure us better than a native medicine man, but he would not be able to tell us *who gave us the disease!*"

We, in the United States or Great Britain, should think twice before we dismiss the primitive beliefs of Africans as nonsense, or laugh at their superstitious customs. In one bazaar I saw a dead parrot on sale as a fetish; disgusting, of course. But we use fetishes like fox tails on our automobiles. We in Brooklyn or Leeds hate to walk under ladders, sit down thirteen at dinner, or light three cigarettes from the same match. Do you ever knock on wood?

Witchcraft is probably increasing, not decreasing, among primitive Bantus at the moment. Many are clinging to their old superstitions even more strongly than before, because of the Western impact which is currently breaking up the old tribal life and destroying ancient customs. They have a double need for personal security, as the security provided by the tribe in older days begins to disappear.

Visitors can see some striking contrasts in the Congo. In one town I saw some horrible things for sale—in a witch doctor's shop an assortment of fetishes like chicken bladders and bubbles made of blown-up sheep's intestines. But on the wall stood a sign printed neatly in English that might have been in a grocery store in rural Vermont: IF YOU HAVE NOTHING TO DO, DO NOT DO IT HERE.

In another town we ran into a pretty girl carrying twins. She wore smears of pale yellowish paint on her forehead, and the babies had circles of the same color —it seemed almost phosphorescent—on their temples. The purpose of this was to drive evil spirits away, since twins are supposed to be unlucky. Most African tribes believe that a double birth is unnatural, and that twins have a curse on them. In fact, until recently in some parts of the Congo twins ran the risk of being killed as soon as they were born. And it was the mother who had to kill them!

Witch doctors wear peculiar costumes, and are often masked. Sometimes they adorn themselves with trophies, such as baboon tails, collected from animals. The chief instruments of the witch doctor are his bones, which are the vertebrae of some animal killed in a special sacrificial manner. To find out what he needs to know or to cast a spell, the witch doctor tosses these bones down, as we play dice, and traces out his message from the design they form.

Most ceremonies having to do with witch-doctoring are secret, and a witch doctor would no more be seen in public in full regalia than would a movie star walk down the streets of Hollywood without any clothes on. Also witch-doctoring is against the law in many communities, and so the witch doctor tries to conceal himself. It is the essence of witch-doctoring that few people in a given region know who the witch doctor really is.

How does a man become a witch doctor? In some places the young man wishing to become one goes out into the woods alone. He lives on berries and nuts, and otherwise submits to a Spartan regime. A period of meditation follows, and then he gets formal instruction from an older witch doctor. Often a son follows his father in the business. The recruit will have to undergo various ordeals. For instance, he may be asked to retire into the jungle until he finds a cer-

tain river, where, armed only with a knife, he must kill a python under water. The python's skin then becomes the most precious part of his regalia. Some witch doctors wear python skins as headdresses. These headdresses can be flung out to a distance of eighteen feet or more.

Africans As Artists

Music and art are a long story. Everybody knows that in recent years primitive African art has strongly influenced contemporary Western painting and sculpture. Wooden figures, bronzes, gold ornaments, and ceremonial masks have won an important place in European and American museums. One characteristic of African sculpture is a bold and violent distortion of limbs and features. Modern French painters do the same sort of thing. But also most African works of art have a very subtle and sophisticated balance of forms.

The motivation of most African art is religious. Masks were made terrifying, because they were created to ward off evil spirits. Fetishes expressed ancestor worship, and many beautiful objects were made originally to be used in tribal dancing, dances which were a salute to the ancestors of the tribe.

Almost everywhere in Africa one senses the deep artistic sensitiveness of the people. In a village market, fruits and vegetables will be arranged on trays so that they make harmonious patterns. Every bit of pepper or grain of corn is put in a special place so that the arrangement is pleasing to the eye. Even individual peas and beans are placed in symmetrical designs, triangles and the like, so that they resemble games that Western children play with marbles. On one Congo road we passed a gang of workmen, breaking rock with picks and hammers. They hammered in unison, *keeping time* as they worked.

African music is based largely on the drum. Few American or European popular songs exist nowadays that do not show the influence of this African instrument with its fierce rhythmic beat. African music is, like art, closely tied up with religious or semi-religious ceremonies. Music is composed as a prayer for rain, success in hunting, desire for children, or the hope to live happily to a venerable age.

Congolese drums are made of wood—logs hollowed out with a slit—or of wood and hide. Elephant's ears are a favorite hide for this purpose. Some anthropologists think that the drum first came into use as a means of driving away spirits of the dead, or, conversely, to summon them. African drums in the forest can be heard over a considerable distance, probably up to seven or eight miles, and relays of drummers can transmit "spoken" messages with astonishing speed and accuracy by a kind of "shorthand." A point a hundred miles away or more can be reached with a message in two hours. Drums never cease beating in some parts of tropical Africa. They sometimes drive white people mildly crazy.

HOW URANIUM FOR THE FIRST ATOM BOMB CAME TO AMERICA

Probably not one American or Englishman in a hundred thousand has ever heard the name Edgar Edouard Sengier. So far as I know no photograph of him has ever appeared in a popular newspaper or magazine, and, although he lived in England for many years and has visited the United States forty or fifty times, I don't think he has ever been interviewed by a ship's news reporter. Edgar Sengier is one of the great unknowns of our time.

This is all the more remarkable because it was Mr. Sengier who made it possible for the United States to make the first atomic bomb. Without Sengier there would have been no bomb—none at least by the summer of 1945, when the bombs on Hiroshima and Nagasaki ended the war against Japan. Of course a great many other people contributed to the atomic bomb project. But if it had not been for Sengier the first bombs would never have exploded when they did, because it was he who produced the deadly uranium without which they could not have been put together and made to work.

What is more, until fairly recently, every atomic bomb manufactured in the United States and tested in Nevada and the South Pacific has been made out of Sengier's uranium, or from plutonium which derives from uranium. Nor would it have been possible to make the first hydrogen bomb without Sengier's uranium, since H-bombs work by means of an atomic trigger made of uranium.

Nowadays uranium is being mined in a good many places—Canada, Colorado, and South Africa. Sengier's uranium is not so indispensable as it was, and several countries produce more uranium nowadays than does the Congo. Nevertheless Sengier's contribution has great historic and dramatic interest.

The Sengier story has never been written before, and it is difficult to write for several reasons. First, Mr. Sengier is an exceptionally modest man. When I met him in Paris he said dryly, "If you are going to write about me, please try to keep me out of it."

Second, security. If it were not for security Sengier would be a household name. During the war and immediately afterward any details about uranium in the Congo were "top secret" to an extreme degree. Even today the Belgians still keep up an extremely hush-hush atmosphere toward uranium.

Uranium aside, Sengier has another claim to fame, because he is as responsible as any man for the development of the great Haut Katanga copper mines. For years he was probably the most important copper-mining magnate in the world.

Sengier, in his seventies now, is chairman of the Union Minière du Haut Katanga. This, as I mentioned in a preceding chapter, is the most powerful single company in the Société Générale, the huge financial and industrial organization which dominates much of the life of Belgium and the Congo.

Sengier was born in Belgium, and was educated to be an engineer. He spent several years in China. When he was about thirty he decided to move on to Africa, and he got a minor job with the Union Minière, which had been created in 1906. The Congo itself only became a Belgian colony in 1908. Elizabethville, the chief city of the Haut Katanga, was founded in 1910. Sengier arrived there in 1911. He, the Union Minière, Elizabethville, and the Congo, all grew up together.

The Union Minière procured in the Katanga area a concession covering 7,700 square miles, more than half the size of Belgium itself. This concession does not expire until 1990. When Sengier arrived, the principal mine was at Kambove, about a hundred miles from Elizabethville. Sengier had to walk there, because there was no other way to reach it. Elizabethville itself was no more than a disorderly nest of tents and tin shanties. I met an old prospector in Elizabethville who shot a rhinoceros forty years ago at the exact spot where the post office stands today.

Slowly, year by year, Sengier rose in the Union Minière hierarchy. The Union Minière overcame fantastic difficulties in building up a mining property in the heart of bush Africa. Nowadays it is one of the biggest producers in the world, not merely of copper and uranium, but of cobalt, zinc, silver, platinum, and many other minerals. Also it has interests in electricity, chemicals, flour mills, housing, transportation, grain, dairying, and water power.

The Union Minière produces 45 per cent of all Congo exports, and I have already mentioned that it provides nearly *half* of the country's total taxes.

Mr. Sengier is a very rich man, but he and his associates live modestly. The whole emphasis is on simplicity. This is part of the Belgian tradition. The guesthouse operated by the Union Minière in Elizabethville is a modest four-room cottage, nothing more. When my wife and I arrived there we found one bottle of milk in the icebox, and nothing else. (Of course more food was forthcoming later.)

Sengier is, naturally, pleased by the immense financial beam and bulk of his company, as well as its success and power. But this is not his main interest. What he looks back to with particular satisfaction is the social contribution the Union Minière has made to the Congo, and above all the improvement it has fostered in race relations.

The Union Minière takes a great deal of wealth out of the country; therefore, as Sengier sees it, it has a duty to put wealth back as well, in order to improve the standard of living of the people as a whole. The copper magnates want a healthy economy for everybody, if only to keep African nationalism down.

The "population" of the Union Minière is about five thousand whites, including wives and children, and about twenty thousand native workers. The Africans do not live in compounds (the prison-like structures which are an ugly feature of the mines in South

Africa), but in well-planned villages. Their housing is quite good by African standards. The cruelty and oppression of the South African system do not exist. No fewer than seven thousand Congolese children go to Union Minière schools, and a strong effort is made to keep them healthy. The hospitals are the best I saw anywhere in Africa. Babies' cribs even have sheets! We visited the clinics, schools, and welfare establishments surrounding the great mine at Kipushi, near Elizabethville, and marveled. Once Mr. Sengier happened to be inspecting this same mine. He exclaimed to his subordinates, "What are we doing here? Producing copper or just babies!"

Union Minière labor policy is complex. The following points might be mentioned:

First, there is no recruiting system like that in the Union of South Africa. Boys are not grabbed out of the bush from surrounding territories and made to work for a certain term.

Second, 90 per cent of the workers are married, and are permitted to live with their families. (This is not allowed in South Africa.)

Third, the wages are not so high as in Northern Rhodesia next door, but social services are more advanced and the physical circumstances of life are good. The Belgians don't believe much in giving too much cash. "The Africans drink cash," our guide in the Katanga said. But the Congo workers get free clothing, food, housing, schools, and medical attention. And, even if cash is not abundant, a skilled worker in the Congo mines can get up to a hundred dollars a month, a very large sum indeed for Africa.

Fourth, an African can rise fairly high, but he must always be under the orders of a white foreman.

Fifth, the Union Minière does not encourage unions. It would be almost impossible for the African workers to organize or make a strike. The contrast to the situation in the Rhodesian mines is very sharp. There African workers do have the right to form their own unions and to strike.

Sixth, there is no "industrial color bar" in the Congo. Whites and blacks work together.

Indeed the principal point to make about labor relations in the Congo has to do with race. The Union Minière is training its black workers to do more complicated work day by day, so that it no longer has to use white men on shovels, cranes, or bulldozers. The blacks have replaced them. This is good business as well as a progressive development, because African labor is so much cheaper than white. By using black labor in skilled fields, the Congo mine owners are able to mine metal more cheaply and make more money.

Our first night in Elizabethville we went to the

fiery Lubumbashi smelter, which has one of the highest smokestacks in the world—492 feet. We could scarcely believe our eyes when we saw African boys handling the huge overhead cranes with their burdens of molten metal, and otherwise doing work of the most difficult, dangerous, and technically exacting sort. The example of the Congo proves that black Africans *can* be trained to do expert white man's work.

One fascinating operation in this realm is the railway that runs from Elizabethville to Ndola in Northern Rhodesia. The railway goes partly on Belgian soil, partly on Rhodesian. At the frontier a white Rhodesian crew takes over from the black African crew. The African crew ran the train in Belgian territory, and ran it perfectly well; it could carry the train on into Rhodesian territory without any trouble at all. It is, after all, the same train. But the white Rhodesians cannot yet accept the fact that a black African is capable of running a locomotive, nor will the white trade union tolerate black competition. So the crews have to be changed.

The Belgians, getting richer every minute because African wages are lower than white, sit back and laugh at this Alice-in-Wonderland situation. So do the Africans. But the ridiculous business of changing the entire train crew when the frontier between the

Congo and Northern Rhodesia is reached has to be gone through twenty or thirty times a day. The black Belgian crews wait patiently at the frontier station and dutifully take the trains back into the Congo after the Rhodesian white crews get off.

More about Uranium

I saw uranium twice in the Haut Katanga. I even touched a piece of ore loaded with it. Then I wanted to wash my hands quickly, out of fear that it might be radioactive enough to hurt. (It wasn't.)

First, we went to the museum in Elizabethville and there, at the entrance, saw on display a block of pitchblende, uranium ore, as big as a pig. It was colored black and gold and looked as if it were covered with a green metallic scum, or moss made of stone. It came from the uranium mine operated by the Union Minière at Shinkolobwe, one of the hardest places in the world to get to. The Belgians won't let anybody approach within miles of it, even today.

Then we saw other lumps of uranium ore. One characteristic of this ore is its savage, morbid color. We saw an ore called tobernite, which is bright yellow-green and silver; fourmarierite (a brilliant marbled orange); sklodowskite (dull black mixed with pea green); kasolite (fawn and gold); saleite (lettuce green); and, most extraordinary of all, something called vanderbrandeite, which is greenish-gray, yellow, black, and orange—all in tiger stripes.

We called on the chief of the Union Minière in Elizabethville, and saw there more samples of this brilliant, hideous ore. One chunk looked like a metal watermelon, pink and green but with flaming veins of lemon and orange. It was difficult to avoid the reflection that rocks like these have fire in them not only by reason of their color, but literally. The fate of civilization depends on a more slender thread than at any time in history because of the strange energies imprisoned in these fiery stones. Rock mined from this remote area in the Belgian Congo is capable of burning up the world.

The uranium mine at Shinkolobwe has a curious history. In about 1915 a lone Belgian prospector, scratching for what he could find, came across some pitchblende, the source of radium. He brought a sample to the local manager of the Union Minière, who said, "Throw it away. I don't want pitchblende. All I want is copper." And, indeed, copper stood at a tremendous premium at that time, in the early days of the first World War.

The prospector, penniless, ended up in London and sold his sample of pitchblende to a secondhand junk dealer who specialized in old minerals and stones. Some months later a Belgian professor of geology, who happened to be on holiday in London, visited this obscure shop in quest of odd stones; he was struck by the pitchblende, bought it, and had it analyzed. It was the richest radium ore he had ever seen or heard of. He took it at once to the headquarters of the Union Minière in London and, as a result, the Shinkolobwe mine came into being.

Shinkolobwe is near Jadotville, which is about ninety miles from Elizabethville. The mine began to produce radium after World War I. First the ore was worked from the surface, by what is known as "open cut mining"; later, as the surface ore became used up, digging for it was carried out underground.

The radium ore was shipped by a sister company of the Union Minière to a plant in Belgium, where it was duly processed. Thus pure radium in very small but important quantities began to reach hospitals and laboratories all over the world.

In those early days nobody thought that the uranium which is contained in ores that produce radium had any particular value. Radium was precious, but there was no known use for uranium. After a time, strangely enough, the Shinkolobwe mine went out of action. The ore containing radium was cheap enough to get, but to extract pure radium out of it was fantastically expensive. A little radium went a long way, and the Union Minière produced it in enough quantity so that, before World War II, there was no point in mining it any more. The market was glutted. So the Shinkolobwe mine was allowed to go derelict and eventually, as underground mines will, it became flooded, and hence incapable of use.

In 1938 Mr. Sengier, then president of the Union Minière, was secretly approached by a British physicist. The physicist told him that German scientists were working intensively on atomic fission, and might soon be able to make an atomic bomb out of uranium. It was therefore of the most urgent importance, the physicist told Sengier, that no uranium should get into German hands, and that the free world should build up important stocks of uranium for future use.

On his own responsibility Sengier proceeded to do something very farseeing and dramatic. He knew that a sizable stockpile of very rich pitchblende ore existed in the Congo, and he arranged to have more than a thousand tons of this shipped from Shinkolobwe to the United States. Secretly, of course. "I did this," he told me, "without telling anything to anybody." The precious ore reached America safely in 1940, and was put in storage in an obscure warehouse in New York. Hence when the American atomic project got under way the essential uranium was already there and available. *Every bit of uranium that went into the first American bomb came from a "mine" above-*

ground and in New York City! Thanks to Edgar Sengier.

This was the first important service that Edgar Sengier rendered the American and Allied cause. Now came another.

The Shinkolobwe mine was, as I have just mentioned, flooded and out of use. The ore in New York would not last forever. American emissaries made contact with Sengier and he met them at a secret meeting place. He did not wait for the Americans to put their questions. In the first moment of conversation he asked abruptly, "Do you want my uranium mine opened, or not?"

They wanted it opened.

Union Minière engineers then proceeded to deflood the Shinkolobwe mine, and soon it was producing uranium again. One stroke of luck helped them. There were large heaps of "tailings," earth and rock that had been mined with the ore years before, but which were thought to be useless, piled round the pit. No one imagined in the old days that these "tailings" had any value, and they had simply been left there. They did not contain radium in big enough quantity to be worth working. But they did contain uranium. And so all these "tailings" found their use.

Very few people have ever visited Shinkolobwe. Only one man, Sengier himself, can give permission to see the mine, even today. During the war the fact that uranium was being mined in the Congo was a dead secret. Shinkolobwe did not even appear on the maps. Now the existence of the mine is public knowledge everywhere, but severe precautions are still taken against sabotage. Luckily Shinkolobwe is easy to guard because it is so isolated; only one road goes there, and this is closely watched.

Three things about uranium in the Congo are still ultrasecret. First, the amount of production. Second, price. Third, how the ore is transported to the United States, although anybody ought to be able to guess this by looking at a map.

When Sengier visited the United States in 1946, President Truman presented him with the Medal of Merit. He was the first non-American civilian in history ever to receive this high decoration. Even though the war was over, the ceremony was top secret, and the record of the proceedings was impounded in the White House for security reasons, because no one wanted it to be known that Sengier had produced uranium from the Congo for America's first bomb. The word "uranium" does not even appear in the citation.

Sengier is a polished man, somewhat stout, with pale skin, white hands, a fringe of white hair, and a short silver mustache clipped with sharp neatness. He conveys a pleasant sense of benevolence and good will—the kind of good will that often comes to a successful man of affairs after his major work is done.

During the war he lived mostly at the Hotel Ambassador in New York City. His telephone rang early one August morning in 1945. Sengier told me, "The voice did not identify itself. But whoever was talking told me to stay close to the radio all that day." He chuckled, "I daresay they thought that I had a right to hear what was going to be announced."

The announcement, from which the world has not yet recovered, was that the United States had exploded its first atomic bomb.

LAND OF THE GIANTS

Ruanda-Urundi, where the Watutsi giants live, is a country like none other on earth. It is a tiny little land, a small splinter of territory situated where the Congo, Uganda, and Tanganyika meet. It fairly boils with color.

But let us put down some cold facts and figures first. Ruanda-Urundi, little known as it is, has the highest density of population (184 per square mile) of any country in Africa, and overpopulation is a serious problem. The density of population in the Congo proper is only 1.8 per square mile. In other words, Ruanda-Urundi is a hundred times more crowded.

Once Ruanda-Urundi belonged to Germany, like

Tanganyika. After World War I German East Africa was broken up; Tanganyika went to the British, and Ruanda-Urundi to the Belgians. But, strictly speaking, Ruanda-Urundi is not part of the Congo and does not "belong" to Belgium. It is almost indistinguishable from the Congo, but legally it is a United Nations Trust Territory, which Belgium merely "administers."

Ruanda and Urundi are separate units historically, but are governed together and are lumped together on most maps; each has about two million people on roughly ten thousand square miles. Of the total of four million people, only 5,406 are white Europeans. About 40 per cent of the total African population is Catholic, and the birth rate is tremendous. Small as this country is, the Ruanda language is the sixth most widely spoken on the entire African continent.

Cattle, as always in Bantu Africa, are important. Although Urundi is a shade bigger, Ruanda has more cattle, and thus is richer. Cattle are the diamonds of the Ruanda people. But the territory has more cattle than it can profitably support, fertile as the soil is. The Ruandans will not kill their cattle for meat (except in special circumstances), and so the cattle population continually gets larger.

Practically all people in Ruanda, even the women, smoke pipes; those of Urundi do not. No anthropologist has ever been able to explain this phenomenon. But the minute you cross the invisible frontier between Ruanda and Urundi pipe-smoking stops. Another difference is that most Urundi women shave their heads; this custom derives from an old-time fear of typhus. Lice, which carry the typhus germ, were apt to get into long hair, and out of fear of typhus the people here came to shave their heads or crop their hair very closely.

Near Astrida, one of the chief towns, we saw women being carried on litters. Dozens of times along the wet red roads men who appeared to be slaves were marching slowly and laboriously up and down the hills transporting these women. I thought at first that the women must be invalids or cripples, but our guide explained that, on the contrary, they were Watutsi noblewomen, who never walk on the roads but are always carried by their servants.

The people of Ruanda and Urundi do not think of themselves as being Congolese or of belonging to the Congo. Their roots are much closer to Uganda and Tanganyika, to the north and east. They are, however, solidly loyal to Belgium, and I had the feeling that many did not even know that, politically speaking, they were wards of the UN. The Belgians, it is hardly necessary to add, don't exactly go out of their way to tell them what their true status is. They want to keep the population as close to Belgium as possible, and would like to merge the whole area with the Congo.

One thing that makes Ruanda distinctive is that it is the home of the celebrated Watutsi giants. Outside the hotel in Astrida, next to a woman cupping a child's head to her naked breast, we ran into the tallest man I have ever seen. He must have been at least seven and a half feet tall.

African nomenclature is full of confusions, particularly in Bantu areas. The correct name of this unique tribe of giants is not Watutsi, but Batutsi. Watutsi is the corrupt Swahili form of the name. Both Watutsi and Batutsi are collective words. If you are referring to a single man, you should properly use the word "Mututsi."

The Watutsi giants have lived in Ruanda for at least four hundred years, and have a dynasty going back eighteen generations. Although very black in color, they are not Negroes. They may be as black as coffins or top hats, but they are not true Negroes. Originally they were a Hamitic people, nomads and cattlemen who lived near the Nile; later these Hamites drifted south and intermingled with the black Sudanese. The Watutsi today startlingly resemble Ethiopians, another people who, even if jet black, are not originally of Negro stock.

The giant Watutsi are the aristocrats of Ruanda-Urundi. They number only about 15 per cent of the population. They are proud, sophisticated, and extremely lazy. Several times we saw Watutsi lords sitting on bicycles, which apparently they did not have the will or energy to propel by themselves. Instead of using the pedals, they were pushed by vassals, the inferior members of the population. The vassals are the giants' slaves.

Most of the Watutsi giants do not look strong, despite their immense height, and give the impression of being much inbred. They have small heads for their height, slim wrists, and delicate, long, thin arms. They live mostly on milk and peas.

They value women highly, almost as highly as their cattle. They condemn divorce, because it breaks up complicated clan and family patterns.

No one has ever explained satisfactorily why the Watutsi are so tall. It is a scientific mystery. There are no other people in the world as tall as these. In any case, tallness is the symbol of racial purity and noble blood.

However, it is important to repeat that only a minority of the Watutsi, roughly 15 per cent, are giants. The rest are mostly of normal stature. Some people think fancifully that these medium-sized folk are the result of interbreeding many generations ago between the giant Watutsi and Pygmies, who live nearby. But this seems unlikely because the Pygmies make up such a small element of the population. Little contact exists nowadays between the giants and the Pygmies.

The King of Ruanda is called the Mwami. His name is Charles Mutara III Rudahigwa. The Belgians consider him to be an authentic monarch, although he has no real power. They refer to him as the King, but when they meet him face to face they adopt the democratic native custom and call him simply "Mwami."

The Mwami is about forty-five, and is very sober in character, even somber. His height is six foot nine, and he is very handsome.

In the Mwami's palace I felt once more the acute contrast between East and West that travelers find everywhere in Africa. The palace is a European building, but it has leopard skins on the floor and ornaments made of the beautiful local basketwork on the walls. The outer walls are decorated with the traditional long spears of the Watutsi, some of which are shaped like harpoons and some like airplane propellers; several look like extraordinary brooms, with steel bristles and fringes. This all seemed to represent African Africa, medieval Africa. Then in the hallway we saw an exercise machine complete with wires

and pulleys that must have been bought in some up-to-date sporting goods store in London or New York. The Mwami uses this to keep in good physical shape. Everywhere in this part of Africa yesterday kisses tomorrow.

The Mwami gave us lunch, and this was the most stupendous meal I ever ate in my life. Belgians are solid eaters, and the Mwami has adopted their eating habits. Just as hors d'oeuvres we had lobsters, shrimps, some delicious Belgian ham, eggs, and asparagus—all in big quantities. Then came a thick steaming soup, and after that chicken in a cream and mushroom sauce. We thought that this must surely be the end of lunch, but no. Servants proceeded to bring in an enormous roast pork weighted down with six or seven vegetables, then a custard for dessert, and finally two inordinately rich cakes. One of these was decorated with rose-shaped ornaments made out of orange ice cream.

I sat next to the Mwami's queen. The meal lasted several hours, but, paralyzed by shyness, she never said a single word. She has not been out in the world much. She has never even been to Usumbura, the capital of Ruanda-Urundi, which is only eighty miles away. Her hair fascinated me. Most Ruanda women of the nobility shave and clip their stiff cones of hair into designs like those you may see on a French poo-

dle with a special carved cut, but the Queen had her hair built up into a solid frizzy pyramid, at least a foot high and shaped so firmly that it was as solid as a hat.

After lunch the male dancers of the Watutsi tribe put on an exhibition for us. This took place in a courtyard in front of the palace, which was lined by a circle of cypresses. Beyond we could see round, thickly cultivated bright green hills.

Watutsi dancing is well known all over Africa, and is a most magnificent and exciting spectacle. The leading dancer, named Rutera, is seven feet five inches tall, and weighs more than three hundred pounds; he is so famous as a dancer and high jumper that his portrait appears on the local banknotes and postage stamps. The dancers carried spears and wore red and white cotton skirts, long-tailed white headdresses of monkey hair and beading, and shimmering bells around their ankles. Watutsi dancers are unique —fluid, violent, and crashingly dynamic. Their chief characteristic is the tremendous jumps and bounds that the dancers have to take. Every Watutsi dancer must be an athlete, specializing in both broad and high jumps.

Part of the movie *King Solomon's Mines* was filmed here, and we drove out to see the royal enclosure and palace built for the film by Metro-Goldwyn-Mayer. It is a painstakingly accurate and elaborate reproduction of the old Watutsi palaces, made mostly of grass with reed porches over the doorways and movable reed walls. It was left intact after the movie was made and given to the people so that they could see how their royal ancestors lived. Of course their own houses today are of the same type, built largely out of reeds in a similar circular form, but they are much smaller and simpler. I noticed that some wooden posts in MGM's royal palace were breaking out into foliage. Already the building is returning to the jungle.

I asked the Mwami if, as in Tanganyika, the people feel a certain sense of freedom and security because the territory is held in trust by the UN. He replied that the UN "made no difference" at all. Belgium is the father. I asked him if there would ever be political parties in Ruanda and he replied simply, "What good do parties do?" I asked him about nationalism, and he scarcely seemed to understand the meaning of the word. Nevertheless the Mwami is not to be discounted as a political force, and the Belgians treat him with great respect, even if he is a puppet.

Urundi also has a Mwami, whose name is Mwambutsa. The Belgians do not give him the distinction of calling him a king, but refer to him merely as Sultan. He is not so tall as the Mwami of Ruanda, and is of less pure stock. He seemed, when we met him, to be cleverer and surer of himself than the Ruanda Mwami, but to have much less nobility and style.

Both Ruanda and Urundi have their native capitals, but the administrative center for the area as a whole, where Belgian control is exercised, is Usumbura. This is a hot, dreary little town on the northern tip of Lake Tanganyika, with a population of about 27,000 black Africans and 3,000 whites.

Here we saw schools, clinics, factories, and hospitals, all of which are a distinct credit to the Belgian system. Usumbura must be the only city in Central or southern Africa with a swimming pool for Africans. The hospital has actual beds, not straw pallets on the floor. But a hearty black lady who had just given birth to a child was nursing it sitting on the floor. She preferred this to the bed, which was empty. Maybe she had never seen a bed before, and did not know what it was for. Anyway she seemed happy.

The Governor of Ruanda-Urundi took us on an expedition. Like all the Belgians, he is a good administrator and he earnestly avoids pomp and ceremony. There was no flag on his car, and we had no chauffeur or other escort. Once we got stuck in the mud, and the Africans who cheerfully helped to pull us out had no idea that the man driving the car was the Governor himself.

The Ruanda-Urundi administration came in for some sharp criticism during a recent meeting of the UN Trusteeship Council in New York. Several delegates said that the Belgians should do more for education, reform the laws restricting the activity of Africans, and make political reforms so that the people would have something to say about writing the laws. One critic of the Belgian system said, "In contrast to what is going on all around it, Ruanda-Urundi is somewhat like a fly embalmed in amber. The system of administration is utterly old-fashioned. In the middle of a sea of rising nationalism, we observe this little island of cautious indirect rule, where the local people merely carry out orders."

On the other hand, Ruanda-Urundi has an Advisory Council on which Africans are represented and the way is being opened to a rudimentary form of elections. The Governor would be delighted to give more Africans political opportunity, but there are very few who are well enough trained or otherwise fit to hold important jobs. We met several of the African councilors, and indeed they seemed to be fifty years behind similar African officials in Uganda or the Sudan, so far as political knowledge is concerned. But the basic reason for this and for other backwardnesses is that the Belgian system keeps education at a minimum, in order to stave off the possibility of later political advance.

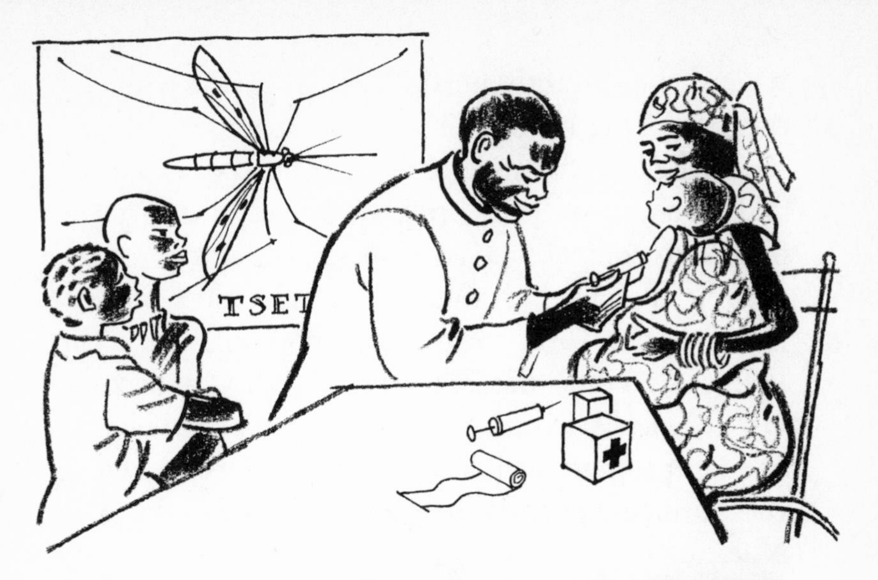

HOPE AND CRISIS IN UGANDA

In London, en route to Africa, I had the great good luck of meeting Winston Churchill at a dinner party, and among other things he said, "Don't miss Uganda!" He described with vivid gusto the source of the Nile at Ripon Falls, with its rapids "flashing like a horse's tail." Later I came across an old book by Churchill, *My African Journey*, published in 1908, in which he counseled the British government of the day, "Concentrate on Uganda."

Mr. Churchill made some remarkable observations in this now forgotten volume, for instance, "What fun to make the immemorial Nile begin its journey by diving through a turbine!" He pointed out that it would be perfectly possible to harness the whole of the giant Nile by building a dam at its source near Ripon Falls in Uganda. Nowhere in the world, he said, would so little brickwork and masonry be needed to control such an immense amount of water. Also he envisaged creating a hydroelectric works.

More than forty years later, in April, 1954, Sir Winston's vision became a vivid reality, when the Owen Falls hydroelectric scheme, one of the biggest and most important development projects in Africa, was formally opened by Queen Elizabeth II. The Nile, for the first time in its history, is being reined and made productive at its source, by means of a giant dam exactly like the one Churchill envisaged.

Uganda—To Begin With

The principal things to say about Uganda, a British protectorate on the northeastern frontier of the Congo, are the following:

1. It is rich. It is the biggest producer of cotton and coffee in the British Commonwealth and, at the moment anyway, prices of these commodities are high. The balance of trade is favorable, something rare for African countries. "If we weren't so well off, we wouldn't be so model," one official told me with a mild ironic smile.

   Uganda has no armed forces to support, which

means that income can be used for other things. There is not a single British soldier in the country. When the Governor needed a new aide-de-camp recently, he had to send all the way to the Royal Air Force in England to get one. Nor has Uganda ever had to spend much money on police; there are only about 250 British police in the whole protectorate—population five-and-a-half million!

2. Uganda is one of the few countries in Africa where the visitor gets the superficial impression that the average African is satisfied with his lot. To eat, all the natives have to do is to reach upward and pluck fruit from the trees. But this generalization, that the people are contented and satisfied, needs to be qualified in several important respects. The Ugandans are a carefree, happy people, but they do not make an altogether tranquil community. Even if they are economically well off, they are politically disturbed. Uganda is seething with political activity, and nationalism is on the march.

As a matter of fact, no African country under European rule can be happy, once it has reached the point of being educated enough to want freedom. And Uganda, unlike the Congo, *has* reached this point. So the people, restless and effervescent, are vigorously demanding change.

3. Uganda has a very complex geographical and political structure. Embedded in the British protectorate are four ancient African kingdoms, which have carefully guarded treaty relationships with Britain. The chief of the four kingdoms, which is also the most important province in Uganda, is called Buganda.

4. Not only is Uganda rich; it is progressive and advanced. The accent, under the British lead, is on *African* development. An African chamber of commerce exists, and so does a credit and savings bank, which lends money to Africans (not whites) at moderate rates of interest. There are eleven thousand African shop owners, a big figure for this part of Africa. A thriving cigarette factory near the town of Jinja, in eastern Uganda, employs African *women* as workers, something almost unprecedented for Bantu Africa. The government does a great deal to train and encourage Africans to do good work in many fields —adult education, road building, safety of water supply, preservation of game, and so on.

The prevailing tone in economic affairs is reformist, liberal, and humanitarian. The country has a ten-year plan, and there are co-operatives all over the place. Electricity is a state monopoly, and so are the railways, posts, and telegraphs.

Government agencies run hotels, the fish industry, various mining developments, and the cement industry.

5. *Uganda does not permit white settlers*, and officially at least there is no color bar. The land policy goes back to 1900. At that time it was thought that Uganda was unfit for European habitation, because of diseases brought by the tsetse fly. So whites were discouraged from settling in Uganda. Even today, no land in Uganda, except a few minor holdings, is owned by white men. Moreover, no white man may buy any land without the express permission of both the British Governor and the local African administration. Hence Uganda has few of the conflicts that usually develop when blacks work on white-owned land, as in Kenya. The chief cause of racial tension, white settlement, does not exist.

Color bar and segregation patterns are hard to describe in Uganda because there are so many variations in custom and habit. There is no segregation in the local buses, schools, shops, or the railroad. Africans are invited, as a matter of course, to important British houses if their official position warrants it, but a few old-style British still refuse to have any social contact with Negroes except at severely official functions. Uganda is probably not quite so free of color bar as the Congo and is certainly nowhere near as free as British countries on the West Coast of Africa like Nigeria or Ghana, but it is much more advanced than Kenya, the Rhodesias, or the Union of South Africa. Moreover, conditions are becoming better all the time. A few years ago Dr. Ralph Bunche, one of the most useful and distinguished of living Americans, was refused admittance to a Uganda hotel. Dr. Bunche is a Negro. He would be accepted without question in Uganda today.

In strict contrast to most of the rest of Equatorial and southern Africa Africans are allowed to drink hard liquor in Uganda—if they are well enough dressed to go into a bar and can afford to order gin or scotch.

Shape, Size, and Qualities of Uganda

Uganda, like the Congo, lies close to the middle of Africa, and is shaped something like a lopsided bucket. It covers 94,000 square miles, roughly the size of West Germany, and has five and a half million people. The population is overwhelmingly African. 99.2 per cent of the people are of Bantu, Nilotic, or Hamitic stock. There are about 50,000 Indians, mostly traders, and only a handful, 7,600, of white Europeans, almost all British. Of this total of 7,600 more than 1,000 are missionaries. Uganda has been a field for Christian missionaries for many years, and about a quarter of the total African population is Christian.

Before proceeding we should mention that Uganda, like Ruanda-Urundi, has some extraordinary peculiarities in nomenclature. Bantu words are very tricky. For instance:

Uganda is the name of the country.

Buganda is the name of the ancient kingdom, now one of the four provinces of Uganda.

Luganda is the name of the language.

Kiganda is an adjective relating to anything that has to do with Buganda.

Muganda is the name for a native of Buganda.

Baganda is the plural of Muganda.

Ganda is an adjective referring to all of the above.

Mostly in this chapter I shall be referring to Buganda, but I will not try to follow the style above too closely.

To the south and west of Uganda are the great unpathed forests of the Congo. To the north is the Sudan where the two countries melt into each other in vast swamps. On the east is Kenya and to the southeast is Victoria Nyanza, the second largest lake in the world, which covers an area the size of Ireland. Below this great lake is Tanganyika, a British domain under UN trusteeship. On the west is the Ruwenzori range, or Mountains of the Moon.

It has been known that these mountains have existed since the second century A.D., but they were not seen by a white man or explored until Stanley discovered them in 1875. They are difficult mountains to climb, because they are almost perpetually smothered by steaming clouds. Uganda is a country both high and swelteringly hot. It can be cold as well. In the Ruwenzori foothills we wore tropical sport clothes by day, but needed heavy blankets at night.

Victoria Nyanza, or Lake Victoria—*Nyanza* means "lake"—is beautiful to look at, but is impossible to swim in or even paddle in safely because of a disease known as bilharzia. This is carried by a tiny parasite that passes part of its life cycle in the body of a variety of snail, which lives in the water. Also, Lake Victoria is full of crocodiles and hippopotamuses. Hippos have been known to roam down the main streets of Jinja at dawn—and Jinja is a Europeanized town with some 7,500 people. Lake Victoria has perils above as well as below its placid surface. We flew over it three times, and I have never known pilots to be more wary in avoiding innocent-looking, but extremely dangerous, thunderclouds.

Uganda has two capitals, Entebbe and Kampala, which are twenty-one miles apart on one of the few good roads in this part of Africa. Until modern times

the journey between them had to be made by rickshaw, and took six or seven hours. Now a car covers the distance in twenty minutes.

Bananas are the staff of life in Uganda, except in the grain country in the north. Our chauffeur leaped out of the car at one village and bought a bunch of bananas which would be his basic food for an entire week. The bunch cost one shilling, or fourteen cents. Banana leaves are umbrellas in Uganda. In the beating rain we several times saw women plodding along the roads, with a broad banana leaf the shape and almost the size of a canoe balanced on their heads. Also bananas are a drink—or rather two different drinks: *pombe*, a beer made of bananas, and *waragi*, a distilled spirit made out of banana juice.

Just as in the Congo, a remarkable feature of the landscape is the procession of huge anthills that dot the sides of the roads. These are jagged and craggy and often reach a height of twelve or fifteen feet, towering like ugly red sentinels and looking like mountains in miniature. Oddly enough the termites or ants living in these fantastic structures contribute some form of chemical change to the earth in them, so that the anthills make exceptionally good material for repairing the roads—earth harder and stickier than normal earth. So, if you need to repair a road cracked by heat or melted down by rain in Uganda, the necessary material is right there.

Some Ugandans eat ants from these fantastic anthills, and think that they are a delicacy, just as Frenchmen eat snails.

Everywhere there are marvels in the realm of vegetation. I don't think I have ever seen any flowers as brilliant as the yellow cassias in Uganda, or the piercingly red plants known as the red-hot poker. On the slopes of the Mountains of the Moon a variety of aster grows seven feet tall.

Also bird and animal life are wonderfully picturesque. I never knew literally what it meant to be awakened early in the morning by the singing of tropical birds until I stayed at Government House in Entebbe. On one drive we passed a sizable town where lions still occasionally walk the streets at night, when they are sure that all two-legged animals are safely in bed. But the fact that Africa is, above all, a continent of sharp contrasts should never be forgotten. For instance, one provincial commissioner on a town on the other side of Uganda told me that he had been in Africa for twenty-three years and had never once seen a lion.

What gives most color to Uganda is, however, not its vegetable or animal life but human beings. Hardly anything in Africa can equal the costumes of the women of Uganda. Congolese women wear bizarrely colorful clothes, but the women of Uganda outdo them. Also the women here are very good-looking, proud, smiling, and serene. They saunter along the roads calmly or cluster in the villages, as graceful as ballet dancers. Their dresses are pulled up by a sash and fall to the ground with a long, lovely sweep. The cloth is not as a rule patterned so vividly as in the Congo, but is made of more solid colors. Rose, orange, violet, and crimson are the favorites.

Years ago in northern Uganda the naked Nilotic savages would usually buy three things first when they got some money, in this order—a hat, an umbrella, and a bicycle. Today, all over Uganda, the things that people want most are sugar, cash for taxes, and cloth to make dresses for their wives. Another sign of advance is that people are crazy about family photographs, calling cards, and football.

There are more than 250,000 bicycles in Uganda, which is an astonishing number; it works out roughly to one for every twenty people in the country. A good bicycle costs about eighty dollars in Kampala. Even children have them; boys go to their fathers and say that they will be humiliated in front of their classmates if they have to walk to school. Of course, this only refers to boys in fairly well-to-do families.

The bicycles are made to support amazing weights,

and whole families mount them. The wife usually rides sidesaddle, with a baby strapped to her back, while her husband works the pedals; another infant may be poised on the handlebar. In Entebbe I saw a woman riding a bicycle while carrying a large pot of banana beer poised on her head. She didn't touch the pot at all. Bicycles can be anything from a truck to a hearse. Corpses are sometimes covered with bark cloth and carried to the cemetery on a bicycle.

The Baganda love to dance, and night clubs outside Kampala must be seen to be believed. A dance "floor" is often no more than a clay courtyard under the trees, and the visitors sit on old crates and boxes. The native name for "dance" is "drama." And, in fact, the dancing of the Baganda is tremendously dramatic. People go into a wild, joyful frenzy, while they gyrate round and round the floor.

American soft drinks like Coca-Cola are big favorites. Several times in Uganda night clubs I saw African boys open Coca-Cola and beer bottles by snapping the metal caps off—with their teeth! Almost all Africans have amazingly strong teeth.

The Baganda are a proud people, much more sophisticated than most of the Congo natives. They are apt to be quite lazy, and incentive is lacking. Even if they do no work, there will probably be enough to eat. They have few social distinctions, and the poorest peasant considers himself to be the equal of the prime minister. Family relationships are extremely complex. Near Jinja we met a chief who told us that his father had two hundred children.

The Two Capitals

Entebbe, the political capital and seat of the British administration, lies on Lake Victoria three miles north of the Equator; several times we crossed this invisible hot line separating the Northern Hemisphere from the Southern. Entebbe was built by the British from scratch, and contains Government House (the residence of the British Governor), public buildings, and the homes of the chief British officials. It has a good hotel, celebrated botanical gardens, and a pleasant atmosphere.

The total white population of Entebbe is only 350. But this little town, so remote and artificial seeming, hidden by foaming jungle and far off the beaten track, is one of the great aerial crossroads in the world. Its airport is one of the best in Africa, and lies almost exactly halfway between Cairo and Johannesburg. So Entebbe is an indispensable stop on most of the transcontinental air routes between Europe and the Cape.

Kampala, the commercial and native capital, is a much bigger town, with a population of 38,000. It has a strong Indian overlay; Indian businessmen and shopkeepers are conspicuous everywhere, and give it an air of vigor and bustle. Kampala is the headquarters of the Buganda government, as distinct from the over-all Uganda administration at Entebbe, and is also the residence of the Kabaka, or native king.

Like Rome, Lisbon, Kiev, and several other cities, Kampala is built on seven hills. One Englishman, taking us for a walk, pointed to the hills and said, "How refreshing it is to see a view in Africa that has an end!" Most of Africa is unendingly flat. An Anglican cathedral stands on one of the Kampala hills, a Roman Catholic church on another, and a Moslem mosque on a third. Religious rivalries have always played a big role in Uganda history, and this even shows in the configuration of the town. The royal palace occupies another hill.

Still another of the Kampala hills has one of the most valuable institutions in all Africa—Makerere College. Until recently, this was the only school with university rank in the whole immense distance between Khartoum and Johannesburg. The official name of Makerere is University College of East Africa, and it is affiliated to the University of London. It was founded in 1922. Not only does it take in boys from Uganda, but from other nearby African territories as well, and gives degrees to about 250 young men a year.

These Makerere graduates have a special status and prestige all over Central, eastern, and southern Africa. It is a great thing to have been to Makerere! Think of what special distinction an American boy would have if he were one of a graduating class of only 250 at the *only* university in the whole Mississippi Valley!

We visited Makerere several times, and I have seldom been more impressed by an educational institution anywhere. Students must be Moslem or Christian. Pagans are not admitted. The boys, and a few girls, come from about eighty different tribes, but they get along well together. Their intellectual curiosity can be vigorous. One recent issue of the school paper contained a lively essay on the evils of witchcraft in seventeenth-century *England*.

Most Makerere graduates go into government service, as doctors, agricultural officers, veterinarians, and the like. The principal merit of Makerere is, obviously, that it gives African boys education and thus opportunity to contribute useful lives to their communities. Also Uganda itself is enlightened by Makerere; the presence of a good educational institution here gives the whole country prestige. What would Cambridge, Massachusetts, be without Harvard, or Oxford, England, without Oxford? The same thing can be said about Kampala.

A Bit of History

The first white man ever to set foot in Uganda was the explorer J. J. Speke in 1854. A few years later, Speke discovered that Victoria Nyanza was the source of the Nile. Other explorers followed Speke. One was Stanley, the first man to travel around the great lake and demonstrate that it was just one body of water, not four or five as had previously been thought. Stanley opened the way for the missionaries who followed by making a compact with the Buganda king of those days, a formidable, bloodthirsty man named Mutesa I.

Not only did the Baganda have a king, but a court, a rudimentary system of justice, a parliament (the Great Lukiko), and a code of chivalry. They had no wheeled transport or written language, but they had existed as a tribe with their own characteristics and identity for almost a thousand years. The royal line goes back for at least four centuries. The Baganda were particularly proud of the fact that they were not naked people, like those near them, but that they wore clothes. They could not weave, but they used cloth made out of the bark of trees. (Some people still wear bark cloth. But it is not very satisfactory for clothing because it is apt to melt down when it rains.)

The missionaries began to arrive in force after 1877, at first British Protestants and then French Catholics. Also Arab traders penetrated the country from the east, and left strong Moslem traces. The struggle for religious power in Uganda was triple. At first the Baganda had no idea at all of what constituted the difference between Catholics and Protestants, but even so many of them became fanatically devoted to their special creeds as soon as they were converted to the Christian faith.

In fact, feeling between Catholics and Protestants became so inflamed that Uganda had a series of bitter, bloody religious wars between 1888 and 1891. Catholic Africans looted and burned Protestant churches; Protestant Africans looted and burned Catholic churches. The Protestants won in the end, but Catholic influence is still marked.

Meantime a great British empire-builder, Lord Lugard, was opening the country up for the Imperial British East African Company. The Baganda say, however, that they were never conquered by force of arms, and are proud of this fact to this day. Penetration by Lugard and his followers was largely peaceable. In 1893 the British government took Buganda over, although many people in London had strong anti-imperialist feelings at the time and opposed this step vigorously. Then the Ugandans were given a treaty by Queen Victoria. The London magazine *Punch* celebrated the signing of this treaty with a famous cartoon which portrayed John Bull looking at a new African baby suddenly deposited in his lap. John Bull's face shows a mixture of doubt, reluctance, and moral satisfaction all combined.

Today Uganda is a British protectorate under a Governor appointed from London, who works with an executive council and legislative council on the spot. There are no political parties in our sense, and there has never been a national election. But, steadily if gradually, the British have given the Africans political leeway and trained them in governmental responsibility, so that they will be able to govern themselves someday. There are no fewer than twenty Africans on the legislative council (parliament), which has a total membership of fifty-six.

Basic British policy is what it is everywhere in Africa, that of preparing Africans by slow—sometimes very slow—stages for eventual self-government. The British cannot go too fast in Uganda because Uganda is split into four native kingdoms, and they claim that effective national unity must be established before self-government can be granted. If unity does not come first, the country might split apart, the

British say. Of course this reasoning serves to give them an excuse for being slow, and nationalist Africans say that the whole argument is spurious.

Until recently, the British thought that they had plenty of time in Uganda, and their reforms were in fact very leisurely. Now they know that time is running out more quickly than anybody could have dreamed a few years ago, and they are confronted with a painful dilemma, which is familiar all over British Africa—whether to give concessions before the Africans are equipped to take full and useful advantage of them, or to put a brake on progress which will stimulate African resentment and provoke unrest.

Things were going nicely in Uganda, on the whole, until a bitter crisis broke out in 1953. Conflict arose between the British Governor, Sir Andrew Cohen, and the Kabaka, or native king, whose name is Mutesa II. The British thought that the Kabaka was showing far too much will of his own and that his behavior was becoming mischievous. So, after a great stir, they took the extreme step of packing him off to exile. But this aroused such passionate resentment in the people that the country all but exploded in agitation, and the Kabaka was later forgiven by London and allowed to resume his throne.

This shows moderation, elasticity, and willingness to admit mistakes on the part of the British which, alas, is not much shared by other colonial powers on the continent. If the Belgians ever dismissed a person of such rank as the Kabaka, assuming that someone like the Kabaka could exist in the Congo at all, it is extremely unlikely that Brussels would ever forgive him and let him return to power, victorious.

In Morocco, the French deposed and exiled Sultan Mohammed V, and eventually he was enabled to return. But this was not because the French wanted to have him back, or changed their minds. His return was forced on them by the pressure of events. Certainly the British make mistakes, but on the whole their rule is much more farseeing and temperate than that of any other colonial power. The gist of their policy is "Give—and keep!"

My wife and I had an interesting meeting with the Kabaka, who is the thirty-seventh member of his line to hold the throne. He is associated with an illustrious tradition, which helps to give him what power he has.

Sensibly, to give the royal blood variety and vitality, a Kabaka is always obliged to marry somebody *not* of royal blood; the Queen must, in other words, be a commoner. A new Kabaka is traditionally

crowned at a holy place near Kampala. Members of the royal entourage are not permitted to cross any water to reach this sacred place because the people believe that water would put a curse on them. So the very streams have to be dammed off for the occasion!

When a Kabaka dies, his widow or widows are obliged, in theory, to live the rest of their lives in total seclusion; they are not permitted to remarry, and must spend their time in what is known as the tomb area, where the graves of previous Kabakas are. The mother of the present Kabaka broke this rule by eloping with an African schoolteacher after twelve years in the tombs. This made such a scandal that a serious political crisis followed, but the lady has been forgiven now.

The present Kabaka is about thirty-two, and is a daintily handsome young man, who looks Ethiopian;

he is very dark, but has an aquiline nose and fine features. His full name is Edward William Frederick David Walugembe Mutebi Luwangula Mutesa, His Highness Mutesa II. He went to school in Cambridge, England, and did well at games. He was not, however, a very serious student. Then he served for a brief time as a captain in one of the British guards regiments. He speaks perfect English, and his conversation often contains phrases like, "My Prime Minister is a most dashing chap!" or, while mingling with guests at a crowded reception, "I say, this is a bit of a squash!"

The Governor of Uganda, Sir Andrew Cohen, an extremely able man with great good will toward Africans and a sincere believer in progress, invited us to attend a special meeting of the Great Lukiko, or native parliament. Here he and the Kabaka made speeches, and this was one of the most vivid ceremonies I witnessed in all Africa. The purpose of the Lukiko session was to announce new reforms whereby the people of Uganda were to be given a larger share in government.

The gathering was marvelously picturesque. The Lukiko meets in what is known as the Royal Enclosure, on top of the Mengo, one of Kampala's hills. This is bounded by a tall fence of elephant grass, and the parliament building itself has a roof of tin, lined with straw. Outside, sitting under the trees, were the drummers. This was the first time I heard African drums really close. The sound is that of an airplane ripping clouds apart. Also the women of the court were squatting outdoors under the trees. They looked like flags draped over lumps of stone—colored magenta, crimson, rose.

Inside, the hall was hung with a galaxy of Union Jacks, and at the far end stood a platform covered luxuriously with leopard and lion skins. Down the aisle marched a dignitary carrying the executioner's ceremonial sword, a moon-shaped blade stuck on a long wooden handle. Then Sir Andrew Cohen entered in a white-gold uniform, the symbol of his authority, and the Kabaka followed him. The Kabaka wore African robes of black and gold, and an attendant held a large purple umbrella over his head, although the ceremony took place indoors.

After the speeches came a reception by the Kabaka in his palace a few hundred yards away. Now the women were allowed to enter the palace, and most of them sat down on the floor. Their skirts spilled on the floor like pools of dye. Aside from red, the two most conspicuous colors were chartreuse and royal blue. Outside, music from the drums still rolled.

Waiters came in bringing punch for the guests. Normally servants are supposed to prostrate themselves in the presence of the Kabaka, but they did not do so this day, no doubt because it would have been difficult to serve European drinks while lying flat on the floor. But I noticed that the four-year-old daughter of the Queen, on being presented to a guest, did not curtsy, but was obliged to *kneel.* We thought that the Kabaka's Queen was a most charming and pretty girl. She is known as the Nabagereka, and she wore a Western frock. A courtier whispered in our ear that her dress had come by air all the way from London. We tried to talk to her, but she was far too shy.

Uganda and the Future

All over Africa people want freedom from the old colonial rule and opportunity to strike out and fend for themselves. Uganda is no exception. More than 100,000 Uganda citizens have joined the nationalist movement, and are agitating steadily for political advance and independence within the Commonwealth.

The British are wonderfully seasoned, expert, and subtle-minded rulers, and they will probably remain in Uganda for a long, long time. But they know full well that the price of European survival on the African continent is reform—more and more reform—and so they will probably do their best to meet the Ugandans halfway in their quest for eventual self-government.

THE WONDERFUL WORLD OF TANGANYIKA

One of the most famous mountains in the world is Mount Kilimanjaro, situated on the border between Kenya and Tanganyika. The word "Kilimanjaro" means "shining mountain" in the local language, and it has some remarkable distinctions. For one thing it is the highest mountain in all Africa; it is more than three and a half miles high. It is about 3,700 feet higher than Mont Blanc, the highest peak in the Alps, and more than 5,900 feet higher than the celebrated Swiss mountain, the Jungfrau.

For another thing Mount Kilimanjaro rises only three degrees away from the Equator, but wears a cap of snow all the year round. That a mountain can be permanently ice-covered in this steamingly hot part of the world makes it doubly challenging. Moreover, Kilimanjaro is not cramped or crowded by other mountains; it is not part of a range but lifts itself out of the earth magnificent and alone. No foothills clutter its smoothly lined flanks, although a mountain named Meru is only twenty-five miles away, and reaches the respectable height of about 14,970 feet.

Kilimanjaro is actually two mountains, not just one. Its highest summit, Kibo, is not a peak but a shallow kind of dome, connected by a long saddle to another summit, Mawenzi. This is a rough sharp peak speckled with black rock. Kibo is the elevation usually seen in photographs and is always clad in snow. Here, encircled by a crust of ice and volcanic ash, is the mountain's giant crater, 6,000 feet across.

The base of the mountain as a whole covers an area fifty-five miles by thirty-five, which should give additional indication of its immensity. It looks like the round back of some stupendous prehistoric monster climbing out of mist, and gives the impression of unassailable might and grandeur.

People who live in the charmed area of Kilimanjaro—both Europeans and Africans—have a strong, almost mystical feeling about it, calling it "the mountain" as if there could be no other mountain in the world. I heard phrases like, "Good chap, the ranger—soundest man with elephants on the mountain!" or "Ghastly bore of a fellow—can't understand what *he's* doing on the mountain!"

Kilimanjaro has produced some splendid native folklore. Parts of the mountain are supposed to have arisen because an African boy, fleeing from an evil spirit, dropped lumps of earth behind him as he ran. This story closely resembles the Greek myth about Atalanta of Calydon, and shows that many of the world's great myths have a common origin.

Kilimanjaro was discovered by a German missionary named Rebman in 1848. People did not believe him at first when he reported the existence of this huge ice-capped peak almost on the Equator. Then other missionaries, government agents, and explorers confirmed Rebman's story, and in 1884 the mountain and its surrounding regions became British territory. Later—the imperialist scramble for Africa was just beginning—it went to Germany. One legend is that Queen Victoria gave it to Kaiser Wilhelm as a birthday present. Whether or not this story is true, the transfer of territory was duly made. Then after

World War I Tanganyika came under British rule again, when the British chased the Germans out.

Kilimanjaro was not climbed until 1889, when a German scientist, Dr. Hans Meyer, made the first ascent of Kibo. The topmost protuberance is still called Kaiser Wilhelm Point, the name given it by Meyer. For many years nobody knew exactly how high the mountain was, and the crater was not fully explored until as recently as 1930. Nowadays Kibo, but not Mawenzi, is comparatively easy to climb. It presents no technically difficult or dangerous mountaineering problems. Expeditions, in fact, go up regularly; the trip takes three days up and two down and costs about fifty dollars. One unusual character, a local American missionary of Russian origin, who has a passionate interest in the mountain, has climbed it no fewer than sixty-five times.

Kilimanjaro gives life. It plucks purple clouds out of the monsoon from the Indian Ocean, makes rain, and carries forests on its back. Rivers flow down its slopes, create magnificent gardens, and become lakes. It is one of the most useful mountains in the world as well as one of the most beautiful and romantic. The leopard made famous by Ernest Hemingway in his story *The Snows of Kilimanjaro* still lies frozen near the summit.

In days of travel I could not get away from Kilimanjaro. We saw it from the most unexpected angles; it followed us like some colossal polar bear breathing out a cold pallid smoke through tropical foliage. Sometimes the clouds would separate just before sundown to expose its bellowed dome—pink, mauve, ivory, and sable. Thin shafts of white cloud usually pierced the top and, if I may change the metaphor, resembled the paper frills on lamb chops.

Many Africans, even those who have been Europeanized, think of Kilimanjaro as God's throne. They pray to it and there is a superstition that a woman must never walk between a man and the mountain. All fertility in the region is supposed to come from Kibo, and when a man dies he is buried facing it.

One person we met and liked near the mountain is Chief Tom Marealle, a thoroughly rational and well-educated young African. He said, "We feel about the mountain the way the British feel about the Thames: it is part of our inheritance, our tradition."

Another chief who was with us challenged Tom. "But even you pray to it, don't you, Chief?" he asked. Mr. Marealle paused a moment and then admitted frankly, "Yes—for rain." Another chief who was present then volunteered, "I pray to it too, but secretly!" Later from another African in the neighborhood I heard a more positive affirmation: "God came from this mountain, and *is* the mountain."

Tanganyika, Its Basic Structure

Tanganyika, a Trust Territory of the UN administered by the British, is enormous. The Kilimanjaro area is only a tiny fraction of the whole. The country has roughly as many thousand square miles as there are days in the year, since it covers just about 365,000 square miles. It is the second largest British territory in all Africa, and among colonial areas in the whole Commonwealth only Nigeria is bigger.

The Kilimanjaro region near towns like Moshi and Arusha is moist and juicy, but most of the rest of Tanganyika is arid, so much so that only about 30 per cent of the land has any use at all. Water, if you could find it, might make the whole territory blossom.

Geologists, I heard it said, should go in for a deep drilling of water exactly as they do for oil. Another factor making part of Tanganyika a waste land—at least as of the moment—is that not less than two-thirds of its total area is infected by the tsetse fly. This brings sleeping sickness, and makes the terrain uninhabitable for cattle.

The spine of the country is the old German railroad that cuts westward from Dar es Salaam to Kigoma. The road system is, for the most part, unbelievably bad. No all-weather road exists at all connecting Lake Tanganyika, which is as big as Holland, with the coast. To drive from Moshi to Dar es Salaam will, with luck, take three hard days, although the distance is only 240 miles; there is not a single garage on the route and no water; there are only two petrol pumps and exactly one hotel.

On Tanganyika's vastness live approximately 8,456,000 people, of whom the overwhelming majority—99.1 per cent—is African. Substantial Indian and Arab (Swahili) communities have deep roots in the country, and so do some Somalis who came originally from the Horn of Africa, far away to the northeast. The white European population of Tanganyika is less than 20,000. Once more we have the spectacle of a thimbleful of Europeans sprinkled like salt over an immense, solid black African mass.

Tanganyika strives as well as it can for compromise, tolerance, and relaxation in racial matters. It is not quite so relaxed as the Congo next door, but is more progressive in such fields as color bar and segregation than Kenya or the Rhodesias. It is, however, not so advanced as French Equatorial Africa which we will visit soon. There are several reasons for the Tanganyika attitude:

1. The European population, although small, is mixed and cosmopolitan. One flourishing community is that of the Greeks, who are far too sensible as busi-

nessmen and otherwise to worry much about color bar. The Greeks actually outnumber the British in Tanganyika, and contribute substantially to the country's worth. Originally they came into Tanganyika as workers to build the railroad.

2. There are some white settlers near Kilimanjaro and several big European plantations exist along the coast, but only 1.3 per cent of the total land of Tanganyika is owned by white men. Hence the problem of white settlement is nowhere near as acute as in other parts of British Africa. Most Britons in Tanganyika are, like the Belgians in the Congo, people who come in as officials or commercial men for a brief period, and who do not intend to stay in the country permanently. The rights of the Africans to their land are carefully safeguarded, as in Uganda, and any transaction involving more than five thousand acres has to go all the way to London for approval. Tanganyika is, in a word, anxious to avoid the mistakes that usually come with white settlement, and which brought tragedy to Kenya; on the other hand, it wants and welcomes some European farmers because they set a good example for the Africans in agricultural methods and in other ways.

3. Tanganyika is a "geographical expression" rather than a nation, and has 120 different tribes. Many

of these are isolated from their neighbors by language and other barriers, and are very primitive; hence there has been little chance for political growth so far. Moreover, most Tanganyikans are peacefully inclined. During the worst of the Mau-Mau crisis in Kenya across the frontier the total number of white troops in Tanganyika was only —thirty!

4. Tanganyika is a UN Trust Territory, and this gives Africans an added feeling of security. But Chief Tom Marealle told us, "The UN is our sheet anchor only because the British co-operate with it loyally. The UN would be worthless if some other kind of government ever came into power."
5. The personality of Sir Edward Twining, who was Governor of Tanganyika until recently and who was an able and progressive administrator, played a big role for a long time. He felt strongly that merit in the community should be based on the work a man does, not on the color of his skin.

Some Tanganyikan Cities

The capital of Tanganyika, Dar es Salaam, with a population of 99,000, is a hot, sticky town on the Indian Ocean. It was built by the Germans, which means that it was built well. The name means "Port of Peace." The atmosphere is largely Arab and Indian, and the mayor is an Indian of partly Arab stock. At the time we were there the municipal council was divided 7-7-6-1 among Europeans, Africans, Asians, and an Arab. Dar es Salaam is prosperous, and inflation is a problem; we were told that the price of a cook for your wife has gone up from 50 to 600 shillings in ten years! The town looks European enough—in spots—but nowhere in Africa are you ever very far from Africa. As recently as November, 1953, several hippopotamuses entered Dar es Salaam from a creek near the airport, and terrorized the whole African quarter of the town.

Dar es Salaam has an enterprising small radio station, which began operation not long ago with little more equipment than a microphone and a blanket hung over a wall; now its programs—in English and Swahili—are heard as far away as Norway. The entire technical staff is African, and its standards are high. Radio has a tremendous future all over Africa. And when TV comes, what fun Africans will have! They possess a marked gift for self-expression, are wonderful dancers, appreciate entertainment avidly, like to act, and have few inhibitions. "We have taken all the joy out of their lives," one high British official told me. "We ignore their tribal dances and try to give them cricket instead. It's awful. We teach them to read, and give them no reading matter that amuses them. The unforgivable sin of British imperialism is not exploitation, but that it has made life so dull."

Tanga, some miles up the coast from Dar, is an interesting small town. The name means "sail," and the population is about 24,000. This is the center of the sisal industry. Sisal is a variety of large daffodil (each plant weighs three hundred pounds) that goes into making rope; it is by far Tanganyika's biggest export, and about 80,000 tons of it go to the United States each year.

What distinguishes the Tanganyika coastal cities like Dar and Tanga from the interior of the country is that the coastal region has a recorded past—a history. Persians, Arabs, Indians, Portuguese have traded on this shore for centuries, and Tanga in particular, like Zanzibar, is the seat of an ancient Arab culture. In a dozen ways the texture of native life here is altogether different from that anywhere else in East or Central Africa. We were startled to see little public cafés along the street, a sight which would be unimaginable in Rhodesia or the Union of South Africa.

Another fascinating town is Arusha on the slopes of Mount Meru, in the neighborhood of Kilimanjaro. It sits at an altitude of 4,600 feet and oddly enough when we visited it it had a population of exactly 4,600 people. On its main street a sign notifies you that Arusha is not only situated in the exact center of British East Africa, but is exactly halfway between Cairo and the Cape. Times of sunrise and sunset do not vary by more than half an hour during the year, because it is so close to the Equator.

Arusha is a polyglot, westernized little town; it has a Greek community, several Germans who pre-date World War I, and some German-Jewish refugees who postdate World War II. Some settlers are South Africans who have been in the area many years; some are recent South African émigrés who hated the Malan government.

Near Arusha is the biggest depot in the world for selling trapped animals to zoos, and the Arusha gardens, under the icy forehead of Kilimanjaro, are of surpassing luxuriance and beauty. But nearby are some desperately poor and primitive communities. The worst village I saw in all Africa was near Arusha; corn here is stored up in the trees, and as a result these seem to be hung with strange-looking nests or baskets. The corn is put up there to keep it out of the reach of giant rats who infest the huts on the ground.

Animals are a lively and colorful problem throughout all this region. Locusts can destroy a farm overnight, and so can a variety of finch called the dioch. One enterprising citizen of the neighborhood invented a novel method of dealing with these finches —he trapped them by dousing his fields with quantities of molasses, on which they stuck. At a sugar plantation on the Pangani River, where the molasses came from, crocodiles are a big nuisance. Our host at one farm proudly showed us a suitcase made out of the hide of a monster crocodile, which was shot soon after it had devoured a Negro worker. "Part of that poor boy must be right here in the skin!" our host said. Nearby is a farm where an eleven-year-old girl gained local celebrity by calling to her mother in a matter-of-fact voice, "Please tell Father that that elephant is in the rose garden again."

On another farm we were the guests of a young man named Johnston, who was a famous Royal Air Force pilot during the war, and who is now a Tanganyika settler. He showed us a most unusual and curious contrivance—two 44-gallon oil drums sealed together with a door at one end and a peephole at the other. In this, lying flat on the ground, Mr. Johnston had lain all the night before waiting for a lion that had been eating his cattle. Bait was strapped to a tree nearby; the lion came; Mr. Johnston shot; the lion—minus one ear—got away.

Moshi, lying at an altitude of 2,900 feet and with a population of 7,500, is the kind of town that

Somerset Maugham, if he ever wrote about Africa, might have invented. Moshi means "smoke"—spume from the mountain. Gardens like those in Arusha are one thing—they are cultivated. Really wet tropical vegetation, such as that which we found in Moshi, is something else again; here the plants literally boil with natural growth.

Moshi is a railway town and has a very civilized look, but under Kilimanjaro's frigid dome it is also a kind of hothouse growing bananas. The banana is the staple food here, as it is in Uganda. People stew, bake, steam, boil, fry, broil, and roast bananas. Bananas make soup, porridge, and even alcohol. Also this versatile fruit is used as a fiber, and a process is being worked out to dry bananas and sell them like figs—also to manufacture banana powder. Another important crop is pyrethrum. This looks like a small chrysanthemum, and is mildly poisonous. It has a soporific effect, and is used all over the world as an insecticide. One favorite local story is of the rhinoceros who wandered by mistake into a patch of pyrethrum, ate some, and at once—all two tons of him—keeled over and went quietly to sleep.

But the real basis of Moshi's life and in fact the economic basis of this whole region is something else —coffee. Some 32,000 African coffee planters are banded together here in what is probably the most successful co-operative undertaking in all of Africa, the Kilimanjaro Native Co-Operative Union, Limited. This is managed by the African growers themselves, with a European secretary, and is a notably successful undertaking. Old-fashioned people who do not think that Africans are capable of handling their own affairs should visit the smart, efficiently run headquarters of this co-operative in Moshi. It has shops, a printing press, laboratories, a recreation center, and better hotel rooms than the Graham Greeneish hotel for Europeans in the town. This organization has given vigor and freshness to the whole community, and opens the way toward what Africa needs above all—the creation of a prosperous middle class.

Some Tanganyikan Tribes

By many people the Masai are thought to be the most "romantic" tribe in all Africa. We encountered our first *Moran*, or Masai warrior, on an upcountry road near Moshi. He carried a tuft of feathers on his spear to indicate that he walked on an errand of peace, and had his face splendidly daubed with red ocher paint. Almost all Masai are tall, well built, and handsome. They are not quite so handsome when they smile, because all of them have two of their front teeth knocked out; one theory to account for this custom is that it enabled a man to eat and drink if he had lockjaw, which in older days was a frequently occurring disease.

The social organization of the Masai is extremely complex, and is based on what are known as "age groups." Each age group is supposed to stick together during life, somewhat like members of a graduating class in an American school or university.

The Masai carry ornaments in their pierced ears, and sometimes these are metal rings a foot or more in diameter. Some wear a disc-shaped bib of beads below the throat, and bind their arms and legs with concentric loops of copper wire. This may come from the nearest telephone pole, if any, and it is often said to be the reason why telephonic communication in the Masai part of Tanganyika is apt to be full of interruptions or broken off.

Sometimes a Masai may wear as much as twenty or thirty pounds of metal and, all in all, the Masai are probably the most picturesquely adorned of all Africans in this general area. Masai women always have their hair closely cropped, like the women in Ruanda-Urundi; the men wear it plaited into a braid until they marry. Sometimes youthful Masai wander into a European beauty shop in Arusha, and stare with envious wonder at the even more complicated way white women do their hair.

The Masai are Nilo-Hamitic in origin, and have a Caucasian cast of feature even if they are jet black. They resemble the Ethiopians and the Ruandans across the Congo border. They have their own highly distinctive language, which is not in the Bantu group, and are contemptuous of education; their children do not as a rule go to school at all.

For a tribe so celebrated, the Masai are comparatively few in number. There are probably only about 100,000 in all, of whom 45,000 live in Tanganyika.

"To get vital statistics about the Masai is the hardest job in this part of Africa," one official told us. The Masai roam over 24,000 square miles in Tanganyika, and have 600,000 head of cattle and another 600,000 sheep and goats; they live by grazing stock, and seldom do any other kind of work. They have been called the "best cattle people in the world."

Another interesting thing about the Masai is their diet. They live almost exclusively on milk and blood from their cattle. The blood is drawn directly from the neck of the living cow through a reed. Sometimes the blood is mixed with milk and sometimes the two fluids together are reduced to a kind of mash. Mostly, however, both the milk and fresh blood are imbibed directly as fluids. The blood drawing is done in circumstances of great secrecy at particular intervals; a British official who had lived among the Masai for five years told us that he had never once seen the ceremony performed. A European doctor whom we met gave it as his opinion that the secret of Masai vitality is their diet. "I could withdraw protein from the Masai, feed them nothing but carbohydrates, and turn them into a much weaker people in no time. Similarly I could make Masai out of other tribesmen if I had enough blood and milk."

The Masai do not even eat chickens, and seldom kill game for food. As a result creatures like zebras and other wild animals are astonishingly tame in the Masai country, because they know that they are unlikely to come to any harm. The Masai do, however, kill lions for fun with spears, and their lion dances are renowned. One object of their lion hunts, aside from ceremony and fun, is to get manes for their headdresses.

The Masai are a fierce, proud, and lonely people, great warriors in the old days, but tranquil now except for their addiction to cattle rustling. They look down on the neighboring tribes, and seldom go into the towns to become clerks or servants. They suffer from a good deal of disease, and as a result the population remains static, which worries some of the elders of the tribe. So the younger Masai have been encouraged lately to marry women of nearby tribes, like the Kikuyu and the Chagga, although they have long had a supercilious attitude toward these tribes. The Chagga, on their side, are wary of the Masai and the best that the Masai can usually get as wives are people much more primitive, like the Waarusha.

What the Masai want most is to be let alone. Yet even these splendidly barbaric tribesmen are beginning to feel the touch of modern times, as is everything in Tanganyika. Because of their wealth in cattle, they have for a long time paid the highest poll tax of any tribe in the country. The government approached them recently with a development plan—largely to improve their water supply and to fight sleeping sickness—and they agreed at once to accept this, although it meant that their taxes would be doubled. It will not be many years before the Masai

drive Fords and Chevrolets, and keep their milk and blood in an electric icebox.

The Chagga (properly, "Wachagga"), who live nearby, are so different from the Masai that it is hard to believe that two such dissimilar people can belong to the same continent, let alone the same small area. The observer is tempted to ask, "What *is* an African, anyway?"

There are about 300,000 Chagga on the eastern, southern, and western slopes of Kilimanjaro; they are an advanced tribe, westernized and sophisticated; they are businessmen, merchants, schoolteachers, clerks, and above all coffee growers; they own no fewer than twelve million coffee trees. Their paramount chief, Tom Marealle, whom I have already mentioned in this chapter and who is known usually as Chief Tom, resembles a Masai warrior about as much as the president of Harvard resembles Tarzan of the Apes.

The Chagga have their own flag, national anthem, and federated organization. They are about 70 per cent Christian. Their tribal council is an important body, and they have their own schools, hospitals, and judicial system. The British are responsible for law and order, since, after all, Chaggaland is part of Tanganyika, but the Chagga are proud of the fact that the local District Commissioners come to their council meetings as "invited" guests. The Chagga even collect their own taxes, and like to say that their budget, around $350,000 per year, is exactly what the budget was in Britain when William the Conqueror came in 1066.

I was much impressed by Chief Tom. This is an able citizen. He is far more cultivated and progressive than any of the Congo chiefs. He speaks perfect English, wears Western dress, and appears to be in his late thirties. He is known as the *Mingi Mkuu* (Big Chief). Members of his family have been chiefs uninterruptedly for thirteen generations. His salary, paid by the Chagga themselves, is £1,800 per year, and he holds office for life. But the appointment is not hereditary. Chief Tom was elected to the paramountcy in 1951, after a lively political fight. The British opposed him at first, not on personal grounds, but because they thought that the institution of paramountcy, which puts one chief above others, was undemocratic. The Chagga had never had a "paramount" chief before.

Chief Tom is not at all anti-British, but he has reasoned and precise views on what is going on in the colonial world. We met him in the office of the KNCU, the Coffee Co-operative. He talked about the land, and how the worst thing about white settlement was not merely that it takes land away from the natives, but forces them into the position of being part of a submerged black working class on white estates. He thinks that the British, for all their good intentions, still govern by a "divide and rule" policy —they deliberately try to keep the tribes apart. He talked a good deal about the position of women, and how vital it was to encourage them to get jobs. He talked, too, about political opportunities in a multi-racial society, and the imperative necessity for development. "Yes. But development *for whom?*" he asked. Chief Tom wants it to be understood that Africans as well as the ruling British should benefit from whatever schemes for development are put into operation in the future.

The British have "pet" tribes. They certainly respect Chief Tom, but they do not really like the Westernized Chagga people. The favorite "British" tribe in these regions is the Masai, even if the Masai are still savages. Or perhaps the British are so fond of the Masai because they *are* still savages. There is always a tendency among old colonials to distrust and dislike educated tribes. The more civilized and emancipated a tribe becomes, the more trouble it is likely to make, because education almost inevitably produces discontent. Similarly in Morocco the colonial French preferred the rude, homespun Berbers to the educated Arabs in the towns.

The biggest tribe in Tanganyika, numbering about one million and a quarter, is the Sukuma. Like the Chagga, the Sukuma have recently formed a federation out of separate chiefdoms—fifty-one in all. Their principal leader is a youthful chief whom I met several times, by name Kidaha Makwaia. He went to Oxford, and was the only African member of the Royal Commission set up in 1952 to study the land problem. Then in 1954 he resigned his chiefdom—an unusual thing to do—in order to go into the government Civil Service. He felt that by doing this he could serve his people better.

Some lively new economic developments are under way in Tanganyika, even in the most remote and primitive areas. In fact, the biggest development scheme in the whole territory is an irrigation project in Sukumuland. The Sukumuland reclamation project will, if it works, raise the living standards of a million people—largely by wiping out the tsetse fly and by improving waterways. Another important development is planned for Gogoland, the "desert" of Tanganyika. Gogoland has more rainfall per year than some of the garden countries in England, but all of it falls in a limited period, and cannot be kept; the problem is to harness and conserve the water. Naturally the motto for work on the Gogoland project is "Gogo Forward."

A Word on History and Politics

Tanganyika is the former German East Africa; it was German, along with what is now Ruanda-Urundi, from the 1880's to World War I. German penetration began with a striking character, Dr. Carl

Peters. Within four months of his arrival on the coast in 1884 he acquired a territory as big as Bavaria, mostly by buying it for practically nothing from the local chiefs. Peters was a private citizen. He planned to sell his tracts to German colonists. He was laughed at in Germany as a visionary. Then quickly the implications of his work became clear to the Kaiser's foreign office, and he was given an Imperial Charter of Protection. The Sultan of Zanzibar, who held theoretical sovereignty over all this territory, was bought off with a grant of £200,000, and the German East Africa Protectorate came into being.

The Germans then spread inland, but they did not completely pacify the huge area they occupied until 1910. One native chief, named Quawa, could not be subdued even after prolonged warfare, and shot himself in 1898 rather than surrender. The Germans took his skull to Berlin as a trophy, and were obliged by a clause in the Treaty of Versailles to return it to Tanganyika in 1919.

In 1903-5 occurred a tragic event, the Maji-Maji rebellion, made chiefly by the Angoni tribe in southern Tanganyika. The Angoni, an offshoot of the Zulus, are a bold and warlike people. They did not like the Germans, and rose fiercely against them. Their movement was in some respects like the recent Mau-Mau rising in Kenya—a desperate struggle against white encroachment on black land, in which political grievances were merged with the worst kind of pagan mysticism and superstition. The Germans put down Maji-Maji with unexampled thoroughness and ferocity. Instead of shooting individual terrorists, they burned crops wholesale, starved villages, and with bloodthirsty efficiency razed the entire countryside. More than 120,000 Africans died. Even today the southern province of Tanganyika, the "Cinderella Province," has not fully recovered from the German terror half a century ago. The economy of the region has never been successfully rebuilt.

German East Africa was conquered by the British, assisted strongly by South Africans and Indians, during the first World War in 1914-18. German exploits during this period, under their formidable commander General von Lettow, were remarkable, but the British won in the end.

Few German traces remain in Tanganyika today, except in architecture. Almost everywhere the *bomas* (government headquarters—literally "fences" or "enclosures"), built solidly and soundly by the Germans in most towns of consequence, are still in use.

Rule by Berlin was not totally a matter of suppression and bloodshed. The Germans (like the Belgians) taught Africans skilled trades and turned them into good carpenters and blacksmiths. Administration of civil law was stern but just. The Germans gave the country what is still the basis of its communication system, and many Tanganyikans of the older generation remember them with respect. Of course the Germans gave the Africans no possibility of advance in politics or the development of nationalism and civil liberty. They were old-time colonial rulers and no mistake about it.

The British paid comparatively little attention to Tanganyika after they took it over in 1918, and ran it for the old League of Nations on what has been called a "care and maintenance basis." In 1938, to buy off Hitler, they entertained the idea of giving the territory back to Germany, but Hitler was after much bigger game and would not accept it.

British policy today is double—to help Tanganyika develop toward self-government, but not too fast. Policy here resembles that of Uganda, but the development is not so fast as in Uganda. The British assert that Tanganyika is nowhere near being fit for self-government as yet, if only because, first, it is still largely a collection of tribes, and second, because the great bulk of the population is still illiterate.

One British remark I heard was, "We are more than eager to let the people here have responsible government—if only to show them how difficult it is to make it work."

Tanganyika, like Uganda, has a strong emerging political party, and nationalism, no matter what the British say, is a growing force. The party is the African National Union (TANU), and its leader is an intelligent and lively man, Julius K. Nyerere, a former schoolteacher. His organization is not as strong as the Uganda National Congress across the border, but it is only a question of time before its strength increases. More and more people in Tanganyika are coming to think of themselves as being "African" instead of as members of separate tribes, and even as "Tanganyikans."

One provincial commissioner told us that, twenty years ago, he would have predicted flatly that any growth of true nationalist sentiment was an impossibility for the country as a whole, no matter over how long a duration of time. "Now I know that I am wrong," he said.

The chief African grievances are a ban on alcohol, the tendency to give more land to white settlers, and, above all, lack of opportunity for education. Mr. Nyerere told an American reporter recently that, under the present program of the government, primary education will not be available to all African children until 1986 or 1990—a shockingly long time.

Every year the Tanganyika government is obliged to submit a long report to the Trusteeship Council of the UN, and sometimes this gets a lively airing. In March, 1954, V. K. Krishna Menon, the Indian delegate, had some pointedly critical remarks to make, although he went out of his way to pay tribute to the good qualities of the bluff and hearty Governor of the time, Sir Edward Twining. Here are some passages from Krishna Menon's speech:

We are too prone to look upon these territories as areas where we are purveying civilization to backward peoples. Here is a territory which has a history going back nearly three thousand years.

There has been little progress toward self-government or independence in this territory. As regards the political aspect of the situation in Tanganyika, there is very little about which we can be happy—except perhaps that there has been no violent conflict. It may be that when there is no violent conflict, there is no progress.

In the field of education, a European child costs the administration £223 a year, an African child costs the administration £8. 5*s*. a year, and an Asian child costs £31 a year. I am sure it is not contended that the European child is so uneducable that it requires thirty times as much effort to teach him. . . .

Early in 1955 the United Nations Visiting Mission to Trust Territories in Africa spent six weeks in

Tanganyika, and issued a striking report. Some of its remarks were unprecedented in UN history. The report noted that millions of Africans are still living on a subsistence economy, recommended important political changes and reforms, and flatly expressed the view that the people of Tanganyika can achieve self-government *within the present generation* on the basis of a political timetable.

The British colonials were profoundly shocked by this document. People in Dar at once called it "biased"—that is, they thought that it was far too pro-African. London took the unusual step of announcing immediately after its publication (and before it was debated in the UN) that its recommendations were "not acceptable to Her Majesty's Government." The British will not countenance any talk of self-government in Tanganyika in the near future, but the rapidly rising Tanganyika nationalists think otherwise and events may well prove that they are right.

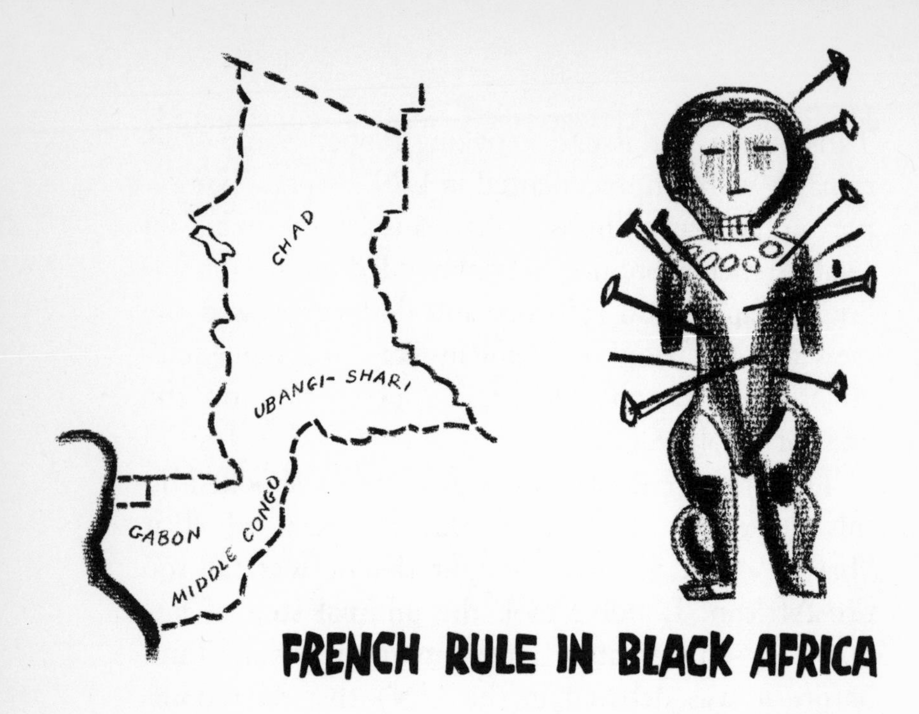

FRENCH RULE IN BLACK AFRICA

Now we turn to the vast expanse of jungle and desert known as French Equatorial Africa, sometimes called FEA for short. The capital of this fascinating region, Brazzaville, is situated directly across the Congo River from Léopoldville. In an earlier chapter I described these two cities as twins, although they differ radically. Much more separates them than the turbid and swiftly flowing Congo.

Léopoldville, in Belgian Africa, might be Jersey City or Leeds, except that it happens to lie in the heart of the tropics. It is businesslike, packed with wealth, bourgeois, proud of its bustle and hurry, and devoid of charm. By contrast, Brazzaville is still predominantly an African city, loosely constructed, colorful, relaxed, with a magic dash of Paris. In Léopoldville everybody works. In Brazzaville everybody—perhaps I should say almost everybody—smiles.

Brazzaville, with about 80,000 Africans and 5,500 Europeans, is substantially smaller than Léopoldville, which has a population of 300,000. Léopoldville was founded by Stanley in 1881; Brazzaville was founded a year later by one of the most romantic of all African explorers, Count Pierre Paul François Savorgnan de Brazza, known as the "father of slaves."

This man, with a tortured, dedicated nature and the ascetic face of a poet, brought 500,000 square miles of Africa to France in two years. Stanley thought that De Brazza was a tramp. The two men were bitter rivals as each raced to acquire territory on opposite sides of the river. De Brazza's first treaties with the native king, by name Makoko, were rudely dismissed by Stanley as "scraps of paper." But they still form the basis of contemporary French rule.

In those days, the 1880's, the technique of European conquest was to get to a place first, plant a flag, and buy off the native chiefs. It was a convenient process, and it went on until almost all of Africa was gobbled up by the European colonizers.

Twin Cities on the Congo

The Belgians in Léopoldville say that Brazzaville is lazy and corrupt, but they like to cross the gummy Congo and have fun there. The French say that Léopoldville may indeed possess the first skyscraper in this part of the world, but that *they* have a real culture, which cannot be measured by the height of buildings. The fact is that Brazzaville is much poorer than Léopoldville, and the French are jealous of this unhappy fact. But the Belgians are jealous too—of Brazzaville's graceful sophistication.

I heard this little story. Crossing on the Congo ferry were two Africans, one well dressed, and the other so shabby that he looked like a scarecrow. The first African was a mechanic in the Ford plant at Léopoldville; the second was a senator who represented Brazzaville in Paris. The senator said, "I am sorry for you, my friend, because you live in political darkness." The mechanic replied amiably, "Yes, but I have clothes on my back."

A Frenchman told us, "Of course we are poorer. On the Belgian side the authorities tell a farmer what crops to grow, or a boy what work to undertake, and if he doesn't obey orders, zip, off he goes to a forced labor gang! Here we cannot do such things. Our Africans have the same rights that we have, and are citizens exactly like you and me."

Then a Belgian told us, "On our side every African gets a square deal, even if he has no political rights. Our District Commissioners speak the local languages, get out into the most remote stretches of country, and really do a job of work. On the French side, everything is neglected. If a native gets into trouble the French District Commissioner will say, 'Learn to speak French, old man, and after you have mastered my language, perhaps I can do something for you!' "

No bridge spans the Congo between Léopoldville and Brazzaville, not even a ferry for heavy material or automobiles. If you want to take your car from Belgian to French territory or vice versa, you must hire a barge. The Congo at this point is about two and a half miles wide. To cross it, from what is called "Le Beach" in Léopoldville to Brazzaville, takes forty minutes in the wet season, twenty in the dry, when the current is not so strong. If your boat, a stubby little river steamer, loses a motor, sirens shriek desperately up and down the river, and a rescue craft sets out at once. Otherwise you may be dragged into the rapids a few miles downstream. Service across the river stops at 11 P.M., and if you are caught on the wrong bank at night, you have to hire a special escorted boat.

Stepping off on the Brazzaville side, you discover what a delight it is to be in France. Paris is 3,700 miles away, but this is Paris, more or less. Emerging from the furiously disorganized customs shed, the first things we saw were a typical French bookshop, a pleasant café with a striped awning and little tables outdoors on a terrace, food stores stocked with bright bottles of wine, and African children who didn't look frightened. French culture is automatically recognizable. It embraces such items as good food, good beds, and good intellectual and artistic tastes.

Brazzaville had an excellent hotel—in contrast to the wretchedly bad hotel in Léopoldville—which is decorated like a modern French liner; the bathrooms are made mostly of aluminium. We had the best meal here that we had had in a hotel for months. But I was more interested in something else. Opposite us at lunch, in what was obviously a fashionable establishment, sat a well-dressed young Negro. And that evening we watched a pretty African girl dine with two white escorts. In other words, color bar, or rather the lack of it in Brazzaville, was the first thing we noticed. This was the first hotel in all Africa where we saw white and black people dining together.

Brazzaville has the most powerful radio station in the French Union; it was built in 1942, and broadcasts in a dozen languages. Its news is picked up and printed in cities as far away as Tokyo. Also in Brazzaville is a highly interesting art school, where African boys straight out of the bush learn how to paint and where they produce works of art which are both primitive and very "modern." And Brazzaville has one delightful night club, to which the African patrons come mostly by bicycle. The girls wear bustles, dance with their shoulders utterly motionless and their hips swaying like canoes in a storm, and have bare feet. Even the waitresses dance while taking your order.

The FEA in General

French Equatorial Africa is shaped somewhat like a boot with a long blunt spike, and covers almost a million square miles. It is three and a half times bigger than Texas, and four and a half times bigger than France itself. It was once called the French Congo. It stretches in a northeasterly direction from the Congo estuary on the Atlantic all the way to the desert frontiers of Libya and the Sudan, almost two thousand miles distant. And what does this enormous mass of territory contain—except emptiness? Four million eight hundred and fifty thousand people (of whom only 25,000 are Europeans); about 300 miles of railroad; 3,000,000 head of cattle concentrated near Lake Chad; a considerable mineral wealth not yet seriously touched; and about forty-six secondary schools, or roughly one for every 96,000 inhabitants. According to a good British authority, only *one* per cent of the total FEA budget went to education until recent years.

French Equatorial Africa is the poorest country in the entire French Union, largely because of the villainous climate and appallingly backward communications. European commercial companies coming in in the early days looted the country. Attempts are now being made to repair the damage to devastated forests, to improve the soil, and to develop scientific agriculture. The chief resources are cotton in the north, and tropical produce like palm oil in the south—also timber, coffee, gold, and diamonds:

French Equatorial Africa (*Afrique Equatoriale Française*) is subdivided into four great territories. Once these were called "colonies," but the word "colony" is now taboo.

Gabon. This, with a population of about 400,000, covers more than 100,000 square miles; it is the most advanced region of the FEA, and comprises most of the coastal area where Africans have been in touch with European influence for centuries. The capital is Libreville, and at a town called Lambaréné is the celebrated forest hospital of Dr. Albert Schweitzer. The city of Port-Gentil at the mouth of the river Ogowé has one of the largest plywood factories in the world —and no hotel. The waters here are full of whales coming up every summer from Antarctic waters. The name Gabon comes from the Portuguese. Many early explorers did notable work in this area. One was a Frenchman, Paul du Chaillu, who discovered the gorilla here in 1856; another was a fabulous English lady, Mary H. Kingsley, who in Victorian petticoats made one of the most dangerous expeditions ever known.

Middle Congo. The capital is Pointe Noire, the area 132,000 square miles, and the population 746,000. Most of the middle Congo is impenetrably wild bush. But Brazzaville is here. Also the Middle Congo has the FEA's only railroad.

Ubangi-Shari. The population is more than a million on an immense, practically unknown area, covering almost 250,000 square miles. The capital is Bangui. This region is an anthropologist's paradise, and contains almost every variety of tropical African oddity. Here natives have their entire bodies, back and front, carved with intricate and symmetrically designed scars, almost like the weaving in an ornate broadloom rug. Here are women with heads squashed and shaped to a point, and, more than anywhere else in Africa, those who wear lip plates—

huge oval protuberances, made of clay or metal, on which the lips are stretched and permanently fixed, so that they look like castanets. Originally these hideous plated lips were a deliberate attempt to disfigure women, so that Arab slave raiders would not carry them off. Then gradually they became fashionable. Nowadays the French regime tries to discourage the custom.

Chad. Chad, with 496,000 square miles, is twice as big as France. The population is about 2,500,000, and the capital is the celebrated frontier post Fort-Lamy. This is a world totally removed from the simmering, green-black Congo swamps and forests; this is dry Africa, Moslem Africa, Saharan Africa, the Africa of chill, moonlike emptiness and desert without end. Fort-Lamy, however, lies on an important body of water, Lake Chad. The first white man ever to reach Chad was a British explorer, the intrepid Hugh Clapperton, who got there in 1832; he was also the first white man ever to see another famous African desert town, Kano in Nigeria.

There are 5,000,000 goats and sheep in the Chad area, and 200,000 camels. Women wear their hair tightly plaited in separate strands so that it lies on the partly naked skull like rows of black beads. Chad is an important military post. Economically Chad suffers from its geographical remoteness and lack of

communications. There are no adequate routes to the sea.

How the French Rule

French policy in Black Africa, as I have already mentioned, is based on the idea of assimilation, that is the gradual—very gradual—absorption of educated Africans, when they become fit, into the realm of

French culture and society. The process will, of course, be a long one since nobody can create a class of African elite—the French call its members *évolués* —overnight, and since it depends above all on education, a field in which French policy has been extremely lax.

The idea of assimilation must, if it is honestly applied, result in the long run in the creation of what sociologists call a "mixed" society. That is, intermarriage between blacks and whites will occur. The French may or may not look forward to this. Their attitude seems to be—let the next generation worry about it. But they are a lucid, rational people, and realize full well, if grudgingly, that something has to be done on a political level now. They are aware that (in French Equatorial Africa as an example) 20,000 Frenchmen cannot rule more than four million blacks indefinitely, without eventual expensive trouble. To this extent they have a much profounder vision than, say, leaders in the Union of South Africa or the white settlers in Kenya and Rhodesia. The French know that, to survive, they have to bring Negroes into the functioning of the state somehow. In any case, French Equatorial Africa—as well as other French territories in Black Africa—has very little color bar, less than we saw in any European territory in our whole trip. As an example, the wife of the French Resident in Libreville told us that her daughter was the only *white* child in the local school.

French policy, even if it gives Africans more political rights than the British do and is much more liberal on color bar, is quite different from British policy. I have said this before, but let me repeat it. The British train Africans for eventual self-government. But the French train them to be Frenchmen. In theory at least, even where their administration is most reactionary, the British have the long-range aim of creating *African* domains within the Commonwealth. The French ambition, on the contrary, is to make their Africa *part of France*. And why not? Is not France the most civilized country on earth? Is not Paris the most shining and splendid of all cities? Should not any African be overwhelmed with delight at the prospect of becoming French? This is how the French argue their case.

Officially, the French do not employ the word "native" any longer, just as they do not use "colony," because these terms are an affront to nationalist-minded Africans. The Ministry of "Colonies" has been replaced by the Ministry of "France Overseas." Instead of "*indigène*" (native) the French use the fancy word "*autochtone*," which comes from the Greek and means "sprung from the land itself."

French policy in Black Africa differs strongly

from Belgian (also from Portuguese and Spanish policy) in that, in theory at least, all Africans in their territories are *citizens of France* itself with all the rights of citizens. In theory everybody is already legally assimilated. The constitution of the Fourth Republic (1946) established complete equality of rights, without reference to race or color, between whites and blacks in all French territories, including the right to vote.

But until 1957, when the first general election was held under universal suffrage, voting was sharply restricted in several ways. Then, on September 28, 1958, came a historic step. General de Gaulle, assuming power, held an election in which all citizens of the French Union were permitted to decide their own future. They were given a choice of several alternatives: (1) to stay as they were; (2) become autonomous republics within the French community; (3) secede from France and strike out on their own as absolutely free, independent states. Only one French territory, Guinea, voted to secede. Most, including the FEA, voted overwhelmingly to become autonomous republics, bound to France but with internal self-government.

It remains to be seen, however, if this "internal self-government" will be truly effective.

French Equatorial Africa, like French West Africa

and other French territories abroad, elects and sends a dozen or more deputies to the French parliament *in Paris*. Most of these are Negroes. No other colonial power permits a phenomenon of this kind. For instance, there are certainly no MPs, white or black, in the House of Commons in London representing Kenya, Uganda, or Tanganyika. No Congolese are members of the Belgian parliament in Brussels. But *all* French overseas territories elect deputies to Paris. This is a strikingly progressive development.

Some critics of French policy think, however, that an embarrassing and even dangerous situation may arise in France as a result of this. At the moment of writing the National Assembly (the former Chamber of Deputies) in Paris has 545 deputies. Of these 80 are from Algeria, the Sahara, and the other Overseas Departments of France, but they debate the laws of *France*. What is more, there would be many more African deputies in Paris if representation were strictly in accordance with population. At present the African deputies in Paris do not, as a rule, vote together. If they did, it is obvious that they could be the balance of power in *French* politics. They could upset the government. A splinter group of Africans might cast the deciding vote on such a thing as whether France, as an example, should withdraw from NATO, or declare war on Russia.

Until recently, most observers did not think that African nationalism could be much of a force in the FEA. The country was too widely spread out and thinly populated, and the Africans were too poorly educated. Moreover, communications were (and are) hopelessly bad, which makes cohesive nationalist expression difficult, and the African population was (and is) split up into hundreds of different tribes.

Nevertheless nationalist spirit is now growing at a tremendous pace, especially since the De Gaulle referendum in September, 1958. Middle Congo now calls itself the "Congo Republic," and Ubangi-Shari has become the "Central African Republic." All four units of the FEA plan, moreover, to federate as soon as possible and become a new independent nation within the French community. France will have charge of defense, foreign affairs, and finance, but otherwise the new country will be autonomous.

On the whole, few Africans in French Equatorial Africa are anti-French, even if they are striking out for full internal self-government. This is what makes French Equatorial Africa and most of French West Africa so different from former French territories like Morocco and Tunisia. The Africans whom the French do succeed in turning into Frenchmen are, on the whole, more loyal to France than British-educated Africans of the same class are to Britain. Most of the African elite in French territories south of the Sahara do not want to break the tie with France, even when they become autonomous. What they want is freedom *within* the general French orbit. They want opportunity and fraternity as well as liberty.

Why is French administration in tropical Africa so much more successful than in Morocco or Algeria? First, the people have been less advanced and therefore easier to govern. Second, the French can afford to take risks at Brazzaville, which is far away, that they could not have afforded to take across the Mediterranean close to home. Third, there are comparatively few colons, white settlers, in most parts of French Equatorial Africa. Fourth, the French have learned a great deal from the lessons of Morocco, Tunisia, and Algeria. Morocco and Tunisia succeeded in wrenching themselves away from French rule, and fierce fighting goes on in Algeria day by day. Naturally France does not want the same thing to happen in Africa south of the Sahara, and consequently is liberalizing its rule.

Bush Flying with the French

We took off from Brazzaville early one morning in thick, sticky fog. We were en route to the Cameroons. I could not believe that any plane of an established airline like Air France would dare to fly in such weather. We walked to the runway and I did not even see our ship until we were ten yards away. Then, it turned out, this was not our ship at all. Ours was a few yards farther on, but still totally invisible. It is an odd experience to get into an airplane you cannot see.

We bucked and burrowed through greasy clouds, with various stops. The flight as far as Lambaréné, where Dr. Schweitzer lives, takes most of a day, although the distance is only a few hundred miles.

The plane, an old DC-3 stripped down to its metal bones, held cargo as well as passengers, and at each stop, depending on what got off and what came aboard, the whole inner structure of the craft was dramatically changed. The cargo was strapped down by canvas belts on metal braces, first on one side, then the other, displacing the folding seats when necessary. I had the sense of being in a structure designed out of movable blocks by some mad child; we were moved around, seats and all, like people in a crazy dream.

An old African wearing orange-colored tennis shoes sat opposite us. He was wedged between a cage of parrots and sacks of grain. He told us that he was a member of the White Fathers. This is a Catholic order devoted to education of the black Africans.

One characteristic of the White Fathers is that all members wear beards, but this old man did not have a beard. He had never flown before, and prayed steadily and crossed himself, moaning gently, as we bumped along. When we put down at a town called Dolisie, he knotted and unknotted his fists with the movement of a heart contracting. I asked him how, since he was a White Father, he could be without a beard.

"I shaved it off last year."

"Why?"

"It scratched."

I asked if this was not contrary to discipline.

He swung his arms gaily. "Discipline? Do you know how old I am? Seventy-five! I was ordained forty-seven years ago, and you talk of discipline!"

The airstrip here, as we looked down, resembled a short green noodle. It has, the pilot told us blandly, the shortest runway in the world. Yet I do not believe there has ever been a serious accident on this wildly difficult run.

After Pointe Noire we became almost totally a cargo plane. I saw something that I have never seen in an aircraft before or since: one of our wing tips became invisible in a mass of steaming cloud, while the other was sharp and clear in flashing sunshine. At another stop we were fueled up by boys using wooden hand-pumps, which worked like cradles. There were no blocks to put behind the wheels; the plane started to blow away, until other boys grabbed the tail and held it. Elegantly, with a gesture of mock despair, the pilot wrung his hands. Everybody in Air France in this part of the world is a d'Artagnan.

Then came Mouila. If ever there was a village lost in the middle of nowhere, Mouila is it. We sat in a dirt-floored reed hut, moist with rot, in an isolated hollow scraped out of the thickest jungle. Then we had lunch. And what did we have for lunch? It was one of the best lunches we had in all Africa, better by far than any I ever had in any airport in the United States. We had a variety of hors d'oeuvres, some ravioli, steak made of buffalo meat, delicious green salad, a good French cheese, and plenty of admirable red wine. And where did all this come from? I do not know!

After Mouila we became a passenger plane again, more or less. We scudded low over lagoons and gray-green muddy rivers sticking into the bush like fat, limp arms and legs. The pilot said that a plane crashing here would instantly be swallowed up by the forest and might quite possibly never be seen again, like a plane falling into the ocean.

Then the terrain became less dense. Rivers spread and oozed out into wet fields. At one town we talked to the European lady who ran the bar. Her husband had carefully marked out a neat little garden with empty beer bottles. I have never seen anything so forlorn. The lady, who had been a nurse, told us that she had recently been poisoned, but had recovered. Tribesmen near a mission station wanted to kill her because she had saved someone else from being poisoned.

Next we skirted three sides of the little rectangle called Rio Muni, which belongs to Spain. French planes do not fly over this "lost" territory, which is also known as Spanish Guinea and which is one of the most backward, derelict regions in the world.

Finally we put down at Douala, our destination. The pilot—who had a face gnarled like the head of a blackthorn—said that Douala was the most difficult airport of his entire experience. "It rains three hundred days a year, it is completely surrounded by rivers, and it has dangerous hills."

Word about the Cameroons

The Cameroons are as interesting as any region in all Africa. Portuguese slave traders dominated the Cameroons first, and gave the country its name, which comes from the delicious little shrimps or prawns (*camerrões* in Portuguese) which are found in its clouded waters. Every time the Cameroons become a political issue in Europe, people who know about this part of the world have been unable to resist making a mild little joke, to the effect that the Cameroons are prawns in the game.

After the Portuguese came the Dutch, and then the British. But British interests were, for most of the nineteenth century, commercial rather than political. The British government was reluctant to annex the Cameroons even though various native chiefs asked for British "protection," that is, inclusion in the Empire. Finally in 1883 a British emissary was sent into the Cameroons to negotiate treaties of annexation with the native kings, in particular one from the Efik country who had the remarkable name Eyo Honesty VII. Another king of the day was called King Duke Ephraim IX of Duketown. Once he called on a British official wearing nothing whatsoever but a top hat.

The British emissary got to Douala just too late. German agents, working in secret, had got in first and had signed an annexation treaty five days before. Indeed those were the days of the "scramble" for Africa!

So the Cameroons were German until the outbreak of World War I in 1914, when a joint Anglo-French invasion team conquered the country. Then they were split between Britain and France under a League of Nations mandate; France got by far the larger share. After World War II the Cameroons, still divided, became a Trust Territory under the United Nations, which it still is. The thin British slice is to the west and has a common frontier with Nigeria; the bigger French slice stretches upward along the borders of French Equatorial Africa toward Lake Chad.

The Germans, although they have been gone for many years, left a strong impression in the Cameroons. Some of their government buildings, put up before 1914, are still the best in the country. German rule was so cruel that thousands of Africans fled; nevertheless the Germans are still respected. Nowadays it is sometimes difficult for the British or French authorities to determine who is the correct chief in a community, because in German times the real chiefs were often hidden to save them from the Germans, whose administration was severe in the extreme; various tribes put up false chiefs to bear the brunt of German discipline or anger. Then some of these false chiefs usurped power, with resultant confusions in the hierarchy that go on to this day.

There are wonders without end in the Cameroons, both in the physical and human spheres. A live volcano called Mount Cameroon, across the bay from Douala, is 13,370 feet high, and is the highest peak in West Africa. The rainfall in one area reaches 400

inches a year, and one sad little town is reputed to be the wettest place in the whole world. One local dignitary, the Fon of Bikon, is supposed to have more wives than any human being in the world, and one tribe has the picturesque name Fang. Red-purple orchids grow in one district to a height of fifteen feet, and in the northern savanna regions there are buildings which wear hats; that is, the grass huts have a small conical roof which fits on the regular roof in the shape of a Chinese coolie's headgear.

The capital of the French Cameroons is Yaoundé, with a population of about 38,000. The economy of its hinterland is rich and varied.

Political fermentation is even more advanced here than in French Equatorial Africa or French West Africa. Legislation is also advanced. The Cameroons have the forty-hour week, collective bargaining, a powerful trade-union movement, and the right to strike. There are several active political parties, and nationalist sentiment is not only vehement but gets stronger day by day. In April, 1957, the Cameroons achieved self-rule in internal affairs, and are scheduled to become completely independent in 1960.

The principal seaport, Douala, is more dynamic than Yaoundé, and is bigger. It has roughly 100,000 people. The overwhelming majority are African. Here, French officials play tennis under yellow fog lights—an odd spectacle—because it is too hot to play until twilight, and twilight in the tropics is very brief. Douala is a flourishing port.

It receives 20,000 *tons* of wine from France every year—for local consumption and distribution inland. We visited one picturesque and noisy night club. It is owned by an African senator, who spent ten years as a headwaiter in a restaurant in the United States.

The Cameroons has only two railways; both were built by the Germans many years ago and have not been much improved since. They are narrow-gauge, and together they span only 315 miles. This in a country bigger than California! I mention this not to emphasize the economic backwardness of the Cameroons, but on the contrary to indicate what a fertile field this part of Africa could be for future development.

Four hours from Douala by launch, twenty minutes by air, is the capital of the British Cameroons, a pleasant old town called Buea. The British Cameroons are not so advanced politically as the French, but social and economic conditions are probably better. The British Cameroons are administered from Nigeria.

Fernando Po—Slave Isle

On a clear day (if there ever is a clear day) you can see the famous island of Fernando Po from the water front of Douala. Few people have ever visited Fernando Po, which belongs to Spain. The Spanish administration is backward, dreary, and corrupt; this is the kind of place where officials shave every fourth day, and are still lounging around in pajamas at 8 P.M.

Fernando Po was named for its discoverer, the Portuguese navigator Fernando Po, who reached it exactly twenty years before another navigator better known, Christopher Columbus, reached the West Indies and discovered America. For a time Fernando Po was called—peculiarly enough—Formosa. The natives of Fernando Po are known as Bubis; the mulattoes, of whom there are many, are called Portos.

Fernando Po does not have enough men to work its cocoa fields, and imports labor from Nigeria. There are about 20,000 Nigerians working here on contract. They get £20 or so for two years' work, and then return to their villages on the mainland with this meager capital. But it may be enough to buy them a wife or a sewing machine, so that they can go into business for themselves.

Fernando Po was, for many years, noted for being one of the most deadly regions in the world from the point of view of health. It was full of malaria and other unpleasant tropical diseases. Also it became infamous as a place where the Spaniards employed convict labor, and the miserable creatures at work here were little more than slaves.

A VISIT TO DR. ALBERT SCHWEITZER

Dr. Albert Schweitzer is one of the most revered men of modern times. Everybody knows that he is a teacher, humanitarian, healer, and practical idealist, and that he has lived as a medical missionary in Lambaréné, a town in French Equatorial Africa, for many years. The breadth of Schweitzer's thought and the force of his ethical sense are almost, if not quite, Olympian. Schweitzer is too lofty to grasp easily; he is a "universal man" in the sense that Leonardo da Vinci and Goethe were universal men.

Schweitzer has had four different professional careers and is an authentic quadruple doctor—in philosophy, medicine, theology, and music. He has written books on Bach, Jesus, and the history of civilization, and is probably the world's foremost authority on the architecture of organs, as well as a foremost interpreter of organ music.

Also Dr. Schweitzer knows a great deal—more than many men who have devoted their lives to these fields—about aesthetics, tropical zoology, anthropology, and agriculture. He loves to work with his hands, and is an expert carpenter, nurse, mason, veterinarian, boatbuilder, dentist, architect, mechanic, pharmacist, and gardener. Universal man indeed!

He has many disciples, and they idolize him. Schweitzer's own view of himself is quite simple. Once he said, "I am a tall tree in the Vosges!" The Vosges are a mountain range near his childhood home.

Schweitzer would be too perfect to be likable if, together with his overwhelming intellectual and moral virtues, he did not have some defects as well. He himself is quite conscious of these, and mentions in one of his books that he has often been "arrogant" and "lacking in love," and that he has even "hated, slandered, and defrauded." In plain fact the old man —he was almost eighty when I saw him—has several frailties. He can be cranky on occasion, dictatorial, pedantic, and bad-tempered. His views on some subjects are obstinately old-fashioned. But, why not? He is a perfectly enormous personality, and personalities so big are bound to be composed of different contradictory elements.

My chief interest was, naturally, to find out something about his relations to Africa. But Dr. Schweitzer does not know much about the Dark Continent except his own small isolated corner. He has worked in Africa, off and on, since 1914, but he has never visited any African country except French Equatorial Africa. (Of course ships on which he was a passenger have made stops at various West Coast ports, and he has seen these briefly. He has never traveled by air.)

Although Schweitzer has lived in Lambaréné for more than forty years, he has never once even been to Brazzaville, the capital of the territory, which is only 420 miles away. This is as though a man should, say, live in Yorkshire all his life, and never once go to London.

As to his attitude toward Africans, this is a mixture of benevolence, irritation, despair, and hope. He has done sublimely good work for Africans, and has been called the greatest living Christian; his heart is good, but he does not seem to have much fondness for the African natives as individuals. Nor does he have much belief in their capacity for self-government, now or later. He hates oppression, of course, and believes profoundly in the brotherhood of man, but he has little conception of the volcanic zest for political advance in today's Africa. With one exception, I do not think he has ever met or exchanged a word with a contemporary educated African nationalist. He is, in short, one of those good old souls who would like to see the white man staying on in colonial areas forever.

Also I was much struck by something else. Dr. Schweitzer is a profound moralist, but he had comparatively little interest in human beings as such, African or otherwise. Basically his interests are art and ideas.

His hospital is run in a manner somewhat difficult to explain. Discipline is extremely strict. Schweitzer seldom talks to those who work for him, and his spiritual aloofness is remarkable.

On the other hand he can be magically charming if he wants to be, and is literally worshiped by his old associates. His laughter, when he laughs, is a striking indication of his inner sweetness. It is a shining laugh, a silvery laugh, and it tinkles.

No bush hospital can be tidy, any more than can a farmyard in South Carolina. There will always be things out of place, with litter on the ground. But Schweitzer's hospital was, I thought, the least well-kept-up place of its kind I saw in all Africa. The sanitary arrangements are primitive. Of course, Schweitzer, an Olympian, is totally above such details. Another thing that struck me was that many of his African workers seemed unhappy and unfriendly —even surly. They wheedled for tips, and seemed dissatisfied with their lot.

One day we watched Schweitzer feed one of his pet antelopes; the hospital area swarms with animals, and on these the doctor bestows the most tender care. He seems to be fonder of the animals in Lambaréné than the human beings, and perhaps they reward him more. The hospital gives a curious atmosphere of being a kind of exercise in penance. Schweitzer is not only saving the bodies of men, but his own immortal soul.

Lifeline of the Great Doctor

Schweitzer was born in Alsace in 1875; his father was a pastor and his mother the daughter of a pastor. The family moved to an Alsatian village called Gunsbach when Albert was an infant, and Gunsbach is still his European home. One of his grandfathers was a schoolmaster and organist, and three of his great-uncles were also organists. Religion and music played a very strong role in the background.

Schweitzer, although a sickly child, performed

prodigies of intellectual vigor from his earliest days. As he grew up he *made* himself master subjects that were particularly difficult for him, like Hebrew. He had a book published by the time he was twenty-three. Long before this his passion for music had expressed itself. He composed a hymn at seven, and began to play the organ at eight, "when his legs were scarcely long enough to reach the pedals."

In early manhood he had three different professional careers which he pursued at the same time. He studied philosophy at the University of Strasbourg, and won his first doctorate with a thesis on Kant. He studied theology at the same time, and in 1900, when he was twenty-five, was ordained a minister. Meantime, he continued his study of the theory of music, and began his professional career as an organist.

At thirty, seeking complete spiritual realization, Schweitzer abruptly changed the whole course of his life in order to study medicine. He determined to go to Africa for the rest of his life as a medical missionary. After seven years of the hardest kind of work he got his M.D., and presently set out for Lambaréné.

Why medicine? Would it not have been enough to have been a non-medical missionary? Because, he says, he was tired of talk and wanted real action.

Why Africa? First, because his father had told him

about the heroism of missionaries there when he was a small child. Second, because he received a communication from the Paris Missionary Society at a critical time in his career, which emphasized the need for medical service in French Equatorial Africa.

Why Lambaréné? Because it was one of the most inaccessible and primitive spots in all Africa, one of the most dangerous, and one without any doctor at all in the area.

Early Days at the Hospital

Lambaréné lies on the river Ogowe, fifty miles south of the Equator, in the territory of Gabon. The easiest way to describe the area where Schweitzer set up his first hospital is to paraphrase the old doctor himself and say that it resembles the beginning of the world—clouds, river, and forest combine and melt into a landscape that seems antediluvian. The air is like steam coming out of a green mist, and I would have not been surprised to see prehistoric lizards rise out of the swamps and swallow whole islets at a gulp.

Lambaréné is situated about 175 miles above the mouth of the Ogowe, and is an island. Farther up the river there is nothing but wild bush. Schweitzer's establishment is not actually on the island, but is a mile or two away on the mainland, across a gray-green, soupy branch of the Ogowe. The population of the Lambaréné area is about two thousand. Of the total forty-four are French.

Every inch of land near Lambaréné had to be seized from the giant forest. The waterways are the roads. The tribesmen in the area had been cannibals not long before. The woods were thick with pythons, gorillas, and other dangerous animals, and the rivers swarmed with crocodiles and hippopotamuses.

Here then, forty-five years ago, Albert Schweitzer began his work. To build a bush hospital from scratch, and Schweitzer did it practically with his bare hands, is something like swimming the Atlantic in a suit of armor. For one period of eighteen *months* he says that he scarcely had time to do any medical work at all.

Once, he records, he threw himself down in despair and groaned aloud, "What a blockhead I was to come out here to doctor savages like this!" Then his faithful African interpreter replied, "Yes, Doctor, here on earth you are a great blockhead, but not in heaven."

Nobody can be more obstinate than an Alsatian theologian. Schweitzer refused to be beaten down. Moreover, despite everything, he came to love Lambaréné, and still loves it profoundly.

Of course Schweitzer has been a great success. When he set out for Africa he thought that he was renouncing his other careers, and giving up forever all that was dearest to him—art and preaching in particular. But as things turned out the old doctor got a good deal out of his sacrifices. Schweitzer has always been able to keep up with his music, and his recordings of Bach, made when he was on holiday in Europe, have been a magnificent success. He lectures and preaches widely whenever he returns to civilization, and has been honored by universities without number. He won the Nobel Peace Prize in 1952, and is certainly one of the two or three most famous men in the world.

First Encounter with the "Thirteenth Apostle"

Nowadays it is easy enough to get to Schweitzer if you do not mind bush flying. I have already mentioned the Air France "milk run" that touches on Lambaréné. We put down at the airport on the bank of the Ogowe, opposite Schweitzer's hospital. I have never seen an airport like this, because there was nothing whatever on it to indicate any connection at all with flying, with the exception of the stepladder on which we descended from the plane. There was not even a windsleeve or a drum of gasoline. When the plane took off, leaving us there, the stepladder remained where it stood, blankly alone in the middle of the field, stepping up to nothing—a perch to infinity.

The effect was very strange. I asked our pilot what Lambaréné was like—not Schweitzer's hospital, but the town. He replied in English, "It stinks." I asked the Negro official representing Air France what it was like. He replied with the utmost solemnity, "It is purgatory on earth, monsieur."

The stout and efficient nurse who met us led us to our room, and gave me the key. She told us to be careful always to lock the door, for fear of theft. She said, "Please never leave your room unlocked, even for a moment." This remark was something of a shock.

Fear of theft is, of course, natural. There are Africans who steal, just as there are Europeans who steal. But Schweitzer's hospital, we found out later, was positively obsessed by fussiness about stealing. It was a sharp disillusion to discover that there should be so much active distrust in a community dedicated to Christianity and good works. Everything at Schweitzer's is kept rigidly under lock and key. The servants are not permitted to carry keys, and we had to give our own key to the room boy every morning when he made up the room.

Our building was a long, low, narrow structure set closely under great trees. Schweitzer designed it himself, and has every reason to be proud of his work. The rooms have cross ventilation, and are cool. The windows are screened, but without glass. There are no closets, bathrooms, running water, or electric light. But every room has a narrow iron bed, a simple washstand, a wicker chair, shelves, and a table. Our room was not only comfortable, but extremely pleasant.

A dozen or more of these narrow cubicles give out on a long shady veranda. Two doors from us was a European woman convalescing from sleeping sickness, who was fondling a parrot. She told us to look out—the parrot was naughty, and might bite. Then we met a young man, one of Schweitzer's assistants, carrying a sick baby monkey. Most of the African servants, I noticed, had bandages stained with a violet disinfectant on their hands or feet. I did not realize at first that they were lepers.

Slop basins from the rooms are poured into an open drain flowing directly in front of the veranda, and bits of bandage and scraps of food are scattered in it. Our guide led us past a nearby rock pile where a dozen Africans were at work swinging hammers. These too were lepers.

We strode up a dirt path, through brush and fruit trees, for a quarter of a mile. There was a sense of aliveness in the very trees: they seemed to vibrate with heavy, hidden life. The path leads to the new leper village which Schweitzer is building. Here, in a ragged clearing, Schweitzer himself came forth. He is a magnificent-looking man, with a powerful aquiline nose, dripping gray moustache, and eyes that really penetrate into you. He is strongly built, and wore an open white shirt, tattered pants, and heavy black shoes. Force, repose, vanity, command, sensitiveness—all these differing characteristics are reflected in his proud, grizzled, piercing face—a wonderful face indeed.

The first thing he did was to ask us, horrified, why my wife and I were not wearing sun helmets. We discovered later that sun helmets are considered absolutely necessary at Lambaréné. Nobody at the hospital ever stirs out of doors by day without a sun helmet, and the venerable doctor himself wears a hat—a crumpled old fedora—even when he goes out at night. At least a dozen times in the next few days people rushed after us every time we stepped out, offering us headgear. Vainly I tried to explain that I had been in Africa for eight months, had visited places much hotter than Lambaréné, and had not worn a hat yet, much less a sun helmet. Then I pointed to the sky. Not a trace of sun was visible. This was June, the dry season in this part of the world, and the sky was heavily overcast with dirty wool clouds; it was an absolute certainty that there would be neither rain nor a single ray of clear sun until August. But

Schweitzer's folk kept pursuing us—for our own good, of course. Sun helmets are archaic in most parts of Africa these days, but not here. There is a good reason for this. The sun helmet is the badge of the old colonial. Also Schweitzer is exceptionally sensitive about sunshine, partly because he had several minor sunstrokes in his youth. When, the next day, he saw that we were still bareheaded, he stared at us as if we must be demented, and then shrugged cheerfully as if to say that the responsibility—if we did get sunstroke—was no longer his.

Schweitzer led us forward briskly to the leper village where he wants to erect structures more substantial than the miserable huts which are there now, and which could be blown away by the next tornado. Immediately he got to work, and it was striking to see him devoting himself to this activity, that of being foreman of a labor gang. But Schweitzer begins and ends each day with this occupation. Somebody has to do it.

A group of lepers stood by. They were, I admit freely, the worst workmen I have ever seen. They used their spades with about as much animation as corpses. If they had spines, the spines were made of blotting paper. They were not too ill to work, but just plain lazy, numb and dazed with boredom and indifference. Schweitzer strode among them, trying valiantly to make them work. He argued, threatened, and cajoled—in vain.

I asked Schweitzer a question or two about the workmen, such as what they got to eat.

"Seven bananas a day."

I asked, "Would they work better if they got eight bananas?"

Dr. Schweitzer's eyes flashed, and they really do flash. "No. That would disturb discipline and morale."

Then we toured the village, smoky with little outdoor fires, and saw ebony children wandering, as if adrift, along paths in the greenish dusk. We passed some bad leper cases, and Schweitzer asked them to show us their hands. "Do not touch the hands," Dr. Schweitzer said.

Hospital in the Jungle

Schweitzer's encampment lies on a low sloping bluff, and has forty-five or more buildings; they are all home-built, simply made, and sturdy. The hospital has between 350 and 400 African patients, and 75 paid African helpers, mostly lepers. There are some 500 mouths to feed every day. The area is heavily wooded, under a canopy of oil palms and mango trees. There are no paved walks or roads. The French authorities wanted to put in a telephone line

to connect Schweitzer with the town of Lambaréné, but the old doctor would not hear of it. There is no running water, no hot water except what is boiled in pots, no electricity (except just enough for the operating room), no motorboat, no automobile, no chapel, and no radio.

Animals drop their refuse everywhere. One afternoon we saw a sick dog lying in one corner of the dispensary. The hospital has about 150 goats, which fertilize the fruit trees. Near the dining hall are a wild pig in a cage and a monkey tied to a tree with a six-foot leash. Four graceful antelopes stand in a rough wire enclosure; the doctor feeds them through the wire after dinner every night. In one cage are guinea pigs and parrots. One European nurse has a pet civet cat, another a big red pig named Tecla, and another a chimpanzee called Fifi. All these pets are treated with the utmost affection and at the same time are made useful, if possible. As we walked in to lunch one day, Schweitzer encountered Tecla, the red pig, and calmly wiped his shoes on her. Obviously the pig enjoyed this process, and her stiff bristles gave the great doctor's shoes a formidable shine.

What appears to be the main hospital ward is a long, one-storied structure, cut apart into narrow dark rooms, each of which opens to a court. The patients do not actually lie on the floor, as they do in most bush hospitals, but on wooden bunks covered with matting. I did not see any sheets or pillows. Outside each door a small smoky fire is burning; here the family of the patient does the cooking. It is good to have these fires, because they keep the mosquitoes down and thus tend to diminish danger from malaria, yellow fever, sleeping sickness, and other diseases. If a man has no family and is too sick to cook for himself, he becomes a serious problem. Most patients will not accept food from anybody not a member of their own tribe, out of fear of being poisoned. A far cry from a medical center in New York City!

Schweitzer has saved thousands of lives, which is the more remarkable considering the primitiveness of most of his equipment. There is, so far as I could see, no mechanism at all for sterilizing bandages under pressure; water has to be boiled in kettles propped up on stones, underneath feeble wood fires out in the open. Things that we take utterly for granted in European hospitals are objects of wonder, if they exist at all. Every safety pin is precious. Schweitzer does not like elaborate modern gadgets. For one thing they are difficult to maintain or repair in a climate as humid as this. What point is there in having rubber hot-water bottles, if they rot in a week? Also Schweitzer wants the Africans to feel comfortable, in circumstances that make them think that they are at home, so that they will not be timid about coming to him if they are ill.

We came across a nurse at work on a sheet of board that served as a makeshift table. Projecting from a blanket was something that looked like the greenish decayed trunk of a small tree. She was scraping blotches of what appeared to be fungi off this. It was a man's leg.

We peered into the operating room one morning; it was startling to be able to look right in from the open courtyard. But the surgery at Schweitzer's is neither rough nor incompetent, despite the surroundings. Medical standards are very high.

In a crowded open space near the dining hall, Africans busily carry produce in rude barrows. Women squat on the ground, binding palm fronds together for roofing; others are busy on sewing machines, and still others iron the wash with primitive irons heated by a lump of wooden coal. The doctor strides back and forth, amid this orderly confusion, seeing that everybody works. The bustle and clatter are that of a frontier camp.

The great moment here comes every day when the rations are distributed. Each African worker is entitled to get seven bananas a day, plus two sticks of manioc wrapped in leaves. Also the ration includes palm oil, rice, and soap from time to time. The bananas (which are really plantains) are measured out with scrupulous care, so that everybody gets fruit of identical size. Some workers get a cash wage as well as their ration, but this is small, averaging only about ten cents a week.

Schweitzer's fruit is marvelous. In our residential hall, when we arrived, I saw a room which seemed to be carpeted by some kind of luxurious pebbly golden rug. It was a layer of grapefruit, put there for storage. Now strangely enough fresh fruit is rare in Africa, except bananas. This is partly because of a native superstition which says that a man planting a fruit tree will die before it bears its first crop—and most fruit trees take a long time to bear. But Schweitzer grows almost every kind of fruit from trees which he himself planted with laborious devotion. One can readily forgive his irritation at Africans who are too stupid or lazy to help him tend his precious fruit trees. Also his vegetable garden is a delight. It is one of his proudest achievements that he has made Lambaréné practically self-sufficient in respect to food.

There are almost always visitors to the Schweitzer camp and some of these, even those who come uninvited, may stay for months or years. Schweitzer's hospitality is boundless, and nobody is turned away. Usually European guests, if they stay any length of time, do some sort of work, like helping to call the hospital roll, or distributing the bananas. African guests are few and far between.

After a day or two we lost most of the instinctive apprehension we felt about lepers. We had already been in contact a dozen times a day with things that had been touched by lepers. To enforce strict segregation of leprous patients or servants would be altogether impossible in a community like Lambaréné. The worst cases are restricted to a certain area, but others wander about quite freely. The truth is that leprosy is not nearly so unpleasant a disease as some that occur widely in our Western world, and it is not particularly contagious. Probably it is less contagious than tuberculosis.

The hospital day is regulated by a series of bells, starting with reveille at 6:30 A.M. Breakfast is at 7:30, and lunch at 12:30. A brief siesta is then supposed to be obligatory. At 6:30 P.M. a bell announces the end of the day; at 7:30 comes the dinner bell, and at 8:30 a final bell, after which Africans are not allowed out of doors. Europeans, too, seldom stir outside after this hour, because of the danger from mosquitoes.

The dining table is long enough to hold twenty or more people and is lit by a row of glowing kerosene lamps. The meals are simple, ample, and delicious. At breakfast pots of tea and coffee are waiting, with toast and several kinds of jam made out of local fruit. At lunch we had a vegetable or fruit stew—for instance, of papaya and carrots mixed together—sweet potatoes, noodles, breadfruit fritters, palm nuts, and steamed bananas. Only once did we have meat. This was some lamb sent over by a neighboring mission. But fish or eggs are served almost every day. At dinner tureens of healthy thick soup are placed on the table as the company assembles, and this is followed by rice, macaroni, other vegetables, and great bowls of magnificent fresh fruit salad.

Schweitzer sits at the middle of the long table, flanked by two of the senior nurses. Gently the nurses offer him special delicacies, like radishes from his preciously tended garden, tidbits of fresh green salad, or brown beans. At each meal, including breakfast, Schweitzer eats steamed bananas. Sometimes he puts his food all together into a soup plate, mashes it up, and eats it with a spoon. When fresh fruit is served, he pulls a large penknife out of his pocket and peels an orange or grapefruit with it.

No meal takes more than half an hour. Immediately before each meal, Schweitzer says a brief grace in French; immediately after dinner he announces a hymn, and hymnbooks are passed around. He walks to an upright piano at one end of the room and plays briefly, but with great vigor, as the company sings; then he returns to his place at the table, slowly opens the Bible, and reads a few lines from Scripture. After dinner doctors and nurses gather at one end of the long room and have cinnamon tea or some similar mild stimulant. Schweitzer may, or may not, join them. Always on leaving the dining hall he takes with him odd bits of food, which he gives to the antelopes. Then, after curfew has descended on the rest of the camp, he returns to his quarters and works until midnight or beyond.

More Glimpses of Le Grand Docteur

Schweitzer saw me writing notes one afternoon, and asked me if I kept a carbon copy of what I wrote. I said no. He said that he didn't either, but that when he is working on a manuscript he writes a message on the first page—"Dear Thief: if you happen by chance to *find* this, please return it to the above address, and you will have my eternal gratitude."

He writes everything in a neat round longhand, and can only find time to write at night, when the day's work is done. Writing is hard work for him, as it is for most authors. Once he boarded a ship carrying with him some unanswered mail. It filled four potato sacks. He has always been scrupulous in keeping up with his heavy correspondence.

He has an extraordinarily alert and broad-ranging intelligence, and his mind is as sharp as a saw; he gives forth opinions with a wonderful sure dogmatism.

He seldom talks much at meals these days—he is too tired—but when he does say something it is worth listening to. Once I asked him, considering his mixed European background, if he thought of himself as being more of a German than a Frenchman, or vice versa. His quick reply was, "I am a man!" Then I asked him what had given him most pleasure in life, and his response was, "Whatever I am working at!"

Schweitzer and the Africans

Africans try Schweitzer's patience sorely, no matter how much he loves them in the abstract. So many of them are shiftless; so many lack any sense at all of responsibility or joy in achievement. He says that his Africans have nothing whatever to do after work is finished each afternoon, but that it never occurs to them to fish in the river—yet they complain of protein deficiency! If they get any education at all, they promptly move into the towns and try to become stenographers. Yet he, Schweitzer, out in the woods, cannot for the life of him find a good carpenter, or even somebody to till a field. He smote himself on the breast telling us this, saying with a booming voice, "I am the only peasant!"

He did not seem to have much faith in the educability of Africans, or even in their good will. He said, "I put a mango here, a banana here, a breadfruit here. The Africans do not know enough to tell which tree is which. I explain. They walk away, and in ten minutes they have forgotten."

But Schweitzer is stating what a good many people would consider to be an extreme view when he says that Africans cannot be trained or educated. Perhaps what he says is true of his own small area, but it is not true of all Africa. The great bulk of Africans almost everywhere in the continent do, if given the chance, yearn for education, appreciate it, and are capable of absorbing knowledge at least to a degree.

To be civilized, Schweitzer thinks, a person—African or non-African—must pass four tests. He must not lie, he must not steal, he must prove that he values property, and he must be kind to animals.

One morning we sat on upturned boxes in the vegetable garden, and Schweitzer gave us a little lecture. Boys passed bearing pails of water. The pails, like much other equipment in the hospital, are sternly marked with initials. Schweitzer saw that the initials were rubbed off one of these pails, and he groaned aloud, "Now they will steal it!" A boy moved very slowly and sloppily at his work. The doctor turned to him with a resigned, exasperated plea, asking him to do better. A moment later he was telling us that the only way to reach the Africans was "through the heart." We climbed toward the hospital, and saw a baby chicken with its eyes scratched out. Schweitzer comforted it tenderly.

On our last night at the hospital we were invited after dinner to accompany Dr. Schweitzer to his small bedroom and adjoining office. This was a great privilege. Here is a mixed-up assortment of books, papers, and tools—a saw was lying across a sheaf of manuscript—empty tins, piles of music, and bits of carpentry. On the wall I saw the portrait of a bearded dignitary—Charles Darwin. It seemed odd that such an iconoclast as Darwin should be here, but Schweitzer explained calmly, "Darwin was a man who sought the truth."

We peeked farther and saw the doctor's favorite antelope, by name Theodore, behind a rude net of wire right there in the room, and two chimpanzees in a cage a few feet away. They are named Romeo and Juliet. Schweitzer sleeps in close proximity to these animals. Then he led us to his celebrated piano. He brought this out with him on his first trip, and has had it ever since. It has organ-like pedal attachments, and is lined with zinc to keep termites out. It weighs three tons, and was presented to him by the Paris Bach Society when he first set out for Africa forty-five years ago.

Schweitzer, my wife, and I all sat squeezed together on the small piano bench. Indeed there was no other place in the room to sit down. Schweitzer played some Bach superbly. This brief nocturnal recital was the last touch, the authentic Schweitzer ceremony of farewell. He was not playing for us particularly. He plays every night, especially when his eyes are tired. He said to one visitor, "I play for my antelope."

But it was a fascinating privilege to hear him play, and it is this picture of him, sitting at that battered old wreck of a piano in the middle of the silent jungle, that I shall always remember as most typical of him—this crusty old Bismarck of the spirit, this magnificent tyrant with a heart of gold.

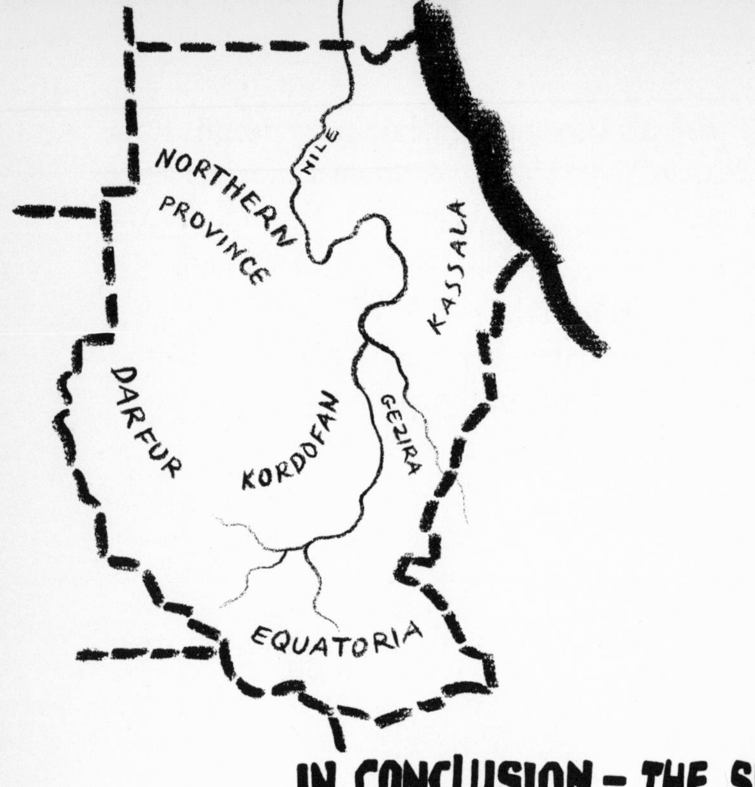

IN CONCLUSION – THE SUDAN

Now, finally, we reach still one more Congo neighbor, the Sudan. This is a country totally different in character and status from any of the others which we have discussed so far. The Sudan is different from the Congo, Uganda, Tanganyika, and most of French Africa for the most elementary, embracing, and important of all reasons—it is free. The Sudanese have won political liberty, and have cast off European rule.

Here in the Sudan colonialism has been abolished. The Sudan is on its own at last as an independent state.

This is part of a strong contemporary trend. Four other African countries have reached independence in the past few years—Morocco, Tunisia, Ghana (formerly called the Gold Coast), and Guinea. There are at present nine independent countries on the continent, not counting the Union of South Africa. They are, in addition to the Sudan and those just mentioned, Libya, Liberia, Egypt, and Ethiopia. Others, like Nigeria, Somaliland, Togoland, and the Cameroons, will reach independence very soon.

What the Sudan Is Like

Politically the Sudan is, I think, the most exciting country we saw in all Africa. This is not a nation half dead at birth, like Libya. It has the intense virility of something not merely newly born but intensely eager to live fully, and its vigorous spirit derives from sound old roots.

The Sudan sounds a note of animation, confidence, and spontaneity. It is full of zest, and sparkles with delight in its new status. I heard a youthful Sudanese say, "Our country is going to be like the United States: we will try to combine here the best of both Africa and Europe." On a different level he went on enthusiastically, "We want more than just good roads, good schools, good hospitals. We want good movies, too!"

Geographically the Sudan is a kind of enormous viaduct between the Mediterranean and African Africa. The Congo touches on it in the southwest, but its most important neighbor is Egypt to the north. Relations with Egypt have dominated most of its history, because of the Nile among other factors.

The name "Sudan" means "Land of Blacks," but plenty of Sudanese are not very black. The country is not to be confused with the French Sudan (a part of French West Africa), which is 2,000 miles away, and which adjoins the Atlantic Ocean. One thing to emphasize is the vastness of the Sudan, its almost measureless immensity. It covers 967,500 square miles, and so is almost four times the size of Texas—if anything can be four times the size of Texas.

There are about nine million Sudanese, and although the country's nationalism is articulate and pronounced it is not altogether easy to define what "a" Sudanese is.

Putting it as briefly as possible, most (but not all) Sudanese are of mixed Arab and Negro blood superimposed on an older Hamitic stock. The distinction is marked between the urban population, about one million, and the tribes out in the desert and equatorial jungle. The bureaucrats in the towns, with their veneer of Western education, often a thin veneer, are apt to despise the nomads and semi-savage tribesmen out in the country. As a matter of fact, man for man, many of the so-called "savages" are far superior to the clerks and officeholders in the towns. They can be splendid specimens physically, and they have their own highly developed standards of conduct, honor, and social behavior.

Moreover, despite their primitiveness, the Sudanese out in the countryside have on the whole a happy way of life. Most are still illiterate, but this does not mean that they are unintelligent. Some of the most famous tribes in Africa are Sudanese, like the Bejas, or Fuzzy-Wuzzys, who spring from the Red Sea area. The Fuzzy-Wuzzys got their name because of their mops of unruly long hair. Among the Nilotic people are the Neurs, the Shilluks, and the Dinkas, about which there could be pages of anthropological description. There are about 820,000 Dinkas and 350,000 Neurs. Most southern Sudanese go in for scarring their bodies in a big way, and in some tribes adolescent boys have their incisor teeth gouged out by spears, as part of a ritualistic ceremony. They are a wonderful people with cattle. Also they have an acute sense of superiority and racial pride. Male Dinkas may occasionally be seen near Khartoum, although their natural habitat is far away to the southwest. They are tall men who customarily, even today, go around stark naked and stand on one foot like storks, supported by long staves.

Long ago, during World War II, I stopped briefly at El Fasher, the capital of Darfur Province in the interior of the Sudan. The surrounding desert looks like a "petrified ocean." This was for a long time regarded as the most remote place in all Africa, the farthest spot from any coast. Darfur covers almost 140,000 square miles, and is nearly as big as Japan. Until 1916 it had its own identity as a semi-independent kingdom. Below is Wau, the capital of the Dinka country. It swarms with big game like elephant and hippopotamus. Another remote and exotic Sudanese town is Malakal, the capital of the Upper Nile province. Here the Shilluks still have their own "king." One chieftain—of the Moru tribe—has the nice name Jumbo.

The Sudan has a favorable balance of trade, and has not had a budget deficit since 1912. There is no income tax. The chief export crops are cotton (by a long way) and gum arabic. Seven-tenths of the total world supply of gum arabic is shipped from Port Sudan. The staple food of the people is dura, a kind of millet.

The Sudan, particularly in its desert regions, is one of the hottest places on the world's surface. Once in April, 1903, a temperature of 126.5 degrees was recorded at Wadi Halfa. Khartoum is the only city I have ever been in—and we visited it in winter—where I could feel heat from the street burn through the soles of my shoes. Egypt and Libya have some unpleasant winds, but nothing to match the *haboob* of the Sudan, which in June blows desert dust as black as smoke from an oil fire over the parched, quivering towns.

Another important point is the influence in much of Africa of the Sudanese group of languages. These, no fewer than 264 in number, have crossed the con-

tinent all the way to the Atlantic coast. Languages spoken by millions of people in Nigeria and the Ghana are Sudanic. Similarly the Nilotic peoples of the Sudan have spread their virile blood far afield, as witness the Masai in Tanganyika and the giant Watutsi, whom we met in Ruanda-Urundi, and who are cousins of the Hamitic Sudanese.

The chief line of demarcation in the Sudan is between north and south. The northerners, who number about 6,500,000, are mostly Arab-speaking, Moslem by religion, and strongly under Egyptian influence. They belong, speaking roughly, to the world of the Levant and the Middle East—even to the world of Europe.

The 2,500,000 southern Sudanese are totally different—pagan, primitive, darker skinned, and with their own native languages. A good many southern tribesmen have, however, become Christianized in the past half century, as a result of stalwart work by British and other missionaries, and many speak Arabic. Antipathy in the Sudan between north and south goes far back, and was once extremely acute. This was mostly on account of slavery. General "Chinese" Gordon, the famous British soldier of fortune, once wrote about Equatoria, the most southerly Sudan province, "When you have got the ink that has soaked into blotting paper out of it, then slavery will cease in these lands." This was written in the 1880's, and Gordon, although right at the time, has been proved wrong by subsequent events. It did not take many years to abolish slavery in the Sudan. Some of the old surviving feudal lords still have family retainers who are virtually slaves, as is the case in several Moslem countries, but organized slavery and the slave traffic have long ago ceased to exist.

In the old days the northern Arabs made periodic raids into the black south, and carried off hundreds of thousands of slaves. The southern Sudan was a kind of reservoir of black man power which the more powerful northerners mercilessly drained. To this day old-fashioned northern Sudanese think of the southerners as "slaves," even if slavery has stopped, and the south still has a lurking subconscious fear of marauders from the north.

Nationalist Sudanese say today that the distinction between north and south is largely artificial, and was built up and made use of by the British to serve their own ends of "divide and rule." In reality, the nationalists say, the Sudan is and always has been an authentic homogeneous unit—politically, economically, and geographically. It is true that the southern languages are different from Arabic spoken in the north, but almost everybody in the south knows English, which is a kind of common language for the whole country. Everything in the southern Sudan flows inevitably downriver (up on the map) to the north, which serves to pull the country together. Certainly it is true that the British, during their fifty years of rule, did not assist north-south intercourse very much. In particular they tried to block conversion of the pagan southerners to Mohammedanism, because they wanted to keep the southern Sudan as a kind of non-Moslem territory to balance the influence of Moslem Egypt in the north. Northern traders were not allowed into the south without a special license, nor could southerners come north. The whole southern area was closed off and kept under its own administration. But quite possibly these maneuvers by the British, even if the Sudanese thought that they were sinister, were an honest effort to protect the primitive southern Sudanese from bad outer influences.

Not only was the southern Sudan a closed area under British rule, so in a manner of speaking was the whole country. Visitors from outside were not encouraged—to put it mildly—to come to the Sudan. When I visited the country recently there were still only four towns in a territory as big as all western Europe which had hotels where Europeans or Americans could stay with any comfort—Khartoum, Wadi

Halfa, Port Sudan, and Juba, the capital of Equatoria. Incredibly enough, the United States was not permitted to have any diplomatic representation at all in the Sudan until 1951; Khartoum, one of the key strategic cities of the world, had no American ambassador or consul. The British wanted to keep outsiders out, just as they tried to keep outsiders out of India in older days.

The Giant and Fruitful Nile

From one point of view the most important thing in the Sudan is the Nile. This stupendous river, at once fixed and elastic, with its swampy roots and flowering Delta, has often been compared to a palm tree, but it more closely resembles the shaft of an esophagus, or alimentary canal, through which the stuff of the Sudan's life passes—also the life of Egypt to the north. The thick, fruitful silt of the Nile Delta near the sea was once top soil in faraway Uganda. Nothing can be more striking than to stand on a bridge in Khartoum, and reflect that the hot, muddy torrent of the Nile consisted originally of Congo snow.

Nobody knows the origin of the name "Nile." It is not the most beautiful or the most spectacular river in the world. But it is the only river about which it may be said that, without it, an entire country would die.

It is also the longest river in the world, measuring 4,116 miles as against 3,988 for the Mississippi-Missouri and 3,900 for the Amazon. For most of its course it is the straightest river in the world as well. Its basin covers 1,100,000 square miles, or roughly one-tenth of the whole of Africa. It loses between a quarter and a half of its total flow before it reaches the Mediterranean, oozing endlessly away into papyrus swamps, or burned up by the fierce desert sun; even so its power, like that of the Congo, remains terrific.

There are several Niles, all part of the same mighty stream. The main branch has its source in Lake Victoria in Uganda, as we know; in a previous chapter I mentioned the great hydroelectric works now in construction at Owen Falls, near its source. Of course Lake Victoria is fed in turn by swift mountain rivers originating in Tanganyika and the Congo. At first the river is known as the Victoria Nile for a short space—there is also an Albert Nile—and then it becomes the *White Nile*. This loops upward into the Sudan and is almost lost for a time in the Sudd swamps, the largest and most impenetrable swamp area in the world. The White Nile then straightens out and flows like a kind of giant pipe through the whole of the Sudan.

The *Blue Nile* rises at Lake Tana in Ethiopia. The two great branches, White and Blue, meet at Khartoum, the capital of the Sudan, to become the main Nile and push northward into Egypt. The White Nile is more sluggish than its Blue sister, and is much steadier. Eighty-four per cent of the total flow of the main Nile comes from the turbulent and dashing Blue. The slope of the *main Nile*, after the junction at Khartoum, is gentle, and is interrupted by a series of celebrated cataracts.

One extraordinary and unique thing about the Nile is that, almost alone among the master rivers of the world, it gets little help from tributaries. About two hundred miles north of Khartoum it is fed by the Atbara, but this is dry for more than half the year. Then, for 1,700 river miles all the way to the Delta, the Nile receives no other stream at all—across a distance as great as the width of the American continent. This is the loneliest, the most self-sufficient, and the most powerful river in the world.

Egypt is made fertile, phenomenally fertile, where it is touched by the magic finger of the Nile, by the remarkable process known as flooding. Once a year the great river swells up like a cobra, rises over its banks, and spills its vast burden of surplus water out into the burning desert. When it recedes the land is impregnated with moisture, that is, life. The Sudan

is not quite so dependent for survival on the Nile as is Egypt, but without the Nile the Sudan could scarcely continue to exist.

To master and harness the Nile further is one of the greatest of all African problems, and obviously involves not only Egypt and the Sudan, but the Congo, Uganda, Ethiopia, and other countries as well. What the Nile needs is a permanent, superscale organization controlling it like the Tennessee Valley

Authority in the United States. But the difficulties are almost insuperable. Communications along the Nile are primitive and far apart. The fact may not be believed, but in the whole of the Sudan the Nile is spanned by only *four* bridges in a total of 2,144 river miles. Moreover, all these bridges are clustered near Khartoum. There is no bridge at all over the Nile between a point north of Owen Falls and Uganda and Kosti, 198 miles south of Khartoum—a distance of almost 3,000 miles!

Two important dams exist in the Sudan, the Jebel Auliya on the White Nile below Khartoum, and the Sennar on the Blue Nile, which fertilizes the Gezira area. Another is to be built soon. One project which could be of tremendous value is a scheme to drain the Sudd swamps, by strangling the Nile into a 186-mile-long canal near Jonglei, in the southern Sudan. Such a canal, by saving huge amounts of Nile water that seep out into the marshland wilderness and are totally lost, could transform the productivity of both Egypt and the Sudan. Ways should also be worked out to store more water on a month-to-month basis, and feed it to the fields as needed. Few problems in the world offer greater challenge to the creative intelligence and good will of mankind.

Egypt has virtually no water except that which the Nile provides, because rainfall is almost non-existent. Since the river flows through the Sudan before it reaches Egypt, Egypt is not only dependent on the Nile but on the Sudan as well for all its water supply. Practically every aspect of Egyptian policy toward the Sudan is based on the absolutely vital necessity of safeguarding its source of water in the Sudan. As a further safeguard, Colonel Nasser, the Egyptian dictator, hopes to build a giant new dam near Aswan, which will be capable of holding and storing the whole of the Nile flood, and which would immensely benefit the Egyptian economy and enrich the entire area. But politics, international politics, has interfered. The United States refused to assist Nasser's project, and as a result Nasser seized the Suez Canal, provoking one of the angriest political crises in modern times.

The Americans opposed Nasser's Aswan project, after first promising him help, largely because Egypt had been flirting with the Communists. Even so, most neutral observers think that the American decision was hasty and ill-advised.

Khartoum and the Gezira

The easiest way to get to Khartoum is from the north, starting from Cairo. The trip, unless you travel by air, takes three stages. The celebrated "white train," which is really a dirty cream color, scuffles out of Cairo every evening with a full complement of European sleeping cars, and reaches Luxor early the next morning. Here you may visit some of the most majestic and melancholy ruins ever made by man, and watch snake charmers seduce cobras out of hidden niches in the rocks. You proceed by train to a town called Shallal near Aswan, and board a blunt-nosed scow, which is really three marine vehicles strapped together. First-class passengers travel in the middle structure, and look down on the dilapidated quarters of those less favored. One of our British friends sighed, "Everything is run by the Wogs now. I can remember when people on these boats dressed for dinner!"

Below Aswan the Nile broadens out to become a sheet of lake. Along the shallow, sandy bank the palms are submerged so that only the tufts show, and the villages along the shores look like a fringe of lace. Shops are mobile—boats with curved sails carrying provisions from dock to dock. At night not a light is visible on the whole river, and the heat most of the year is positively infernal.

At Wadi Halfa you enter the Sudan and board a train again for the third stage of the journey. This train was regarded by most of the British who used to live proudly in the Sudan as the best in the world, and indeed it is still extraordinarily good. You learn now (if you have not already learned it) that this is a hot country. The train is fawn-colored, with roomy compartments like those on Indian trains, in order to provide as much air as possible; there are only seven windows to a car, and these are glassed in blue and shuttered heavily, to keep the fierce sunshine out.

The run from Wadi Halfa to Khartoum takes twenty-seven hours. The train cuts straight across the desert, and then winds its way along the Nile. The desert stations do not have names, but only numbers, and stand exactly fifty miles apart. The station-masters are Greek; one reason for this is supposed to be that no other people could stand the loneliness.

The most famous stop is No. 6, because it has water. At all the others, water for the trains has to be brought in—by train! Each station has a cluster of conical brick huts where the local personnel live; the huts are pure white to deflect the sun, and have dead-black caps.

At once, descending at these stations and watching people, you feel an acute sense of the profound difference between the Sudan and some of the surrounding countries. Buildings are better kept up. Children are cleanly dressed and have fewer sores; veiled women wear pure-white flowing robes and do not beg. The whole impression is one of dignity, sturdiness, and pride.

Khartoum, pivotal to the future of all Africa, is actually three cities—Khartoum itself (population 79,000) which is largely devoted to government; Khartoum North (41,000), an industrial suburb; and Omdurman (128,000) across the river, which is the Arab town. The name "Khartoum" means "Elephant's trunk."

Khartoum was founded by the Egyptians in 1823, destroyed by fierce Sudanese dervishes in the 1880's, and rebuilt by the British general Lord Kitchener in 1899. He laid it out—with magnificent old-style self-righteousness and confidence!—in the shape of a Union Jack. This served a good tactical purpose, since machine guns could easily command the long, slanting streets with their numerous intersections, but it certainly seems to be an anachronism now. Also it makes for difficult traffic problems.

Khartoum's chief distinction is that it lies at the confluence of the Blue and White Nile. Winston Churchill once described the city as a "spout." I was much impressed by the lights over the big bridge—some white, some blue—but this has no deliberate symbolic significance. The White Nile may be whitish, if not actually white, at Khartoum, but the Blue is a dirty brownish color.

The two rivers maintain their separate identities for miles after they leave Khartoum, even though they have become parts of the same thick stream. You can see each current. Swimming is possible in the river near Khartoum because heavy steamboat traffic has frightened away the crocodiles. Danger remains, however, from bilharzia, the sinister disease carried by river snails.

Khartoum is the seat of University College. This is an amalgamation of the Kitchener School of Medicine and one of the most renowned of all institutions of learning in Africa, Gordon Memorial College. It gives degrees honored by the University of London, and is the only school of such standing in the whole of eastern or Central Africa except Makerere in Uganda. The United Kingdom recently gave its endowment fund a free gift of one million pounds in recognition of the Sudanese contribution to the Allied cause in World War II. There are five hundred students taking degrees in law, medicine, public administration, engineering, and agriculture. The college has no official connection with the Sudanese government, but no government at all would be possible without it, because it trains the governing class. Here, under British tutelage, Sudanese youth received its higher education for half a century. It is a striking irony that practically all students turned out by Gordon College became vigorous nationalists. By fostering an institution of this kind, the British, a phenomenally puzzling people, deliberately planted the seeds of their own doom. For now nationalism has won, and they are out.

Omdurman, across the Nile on the western bank, was built as a modern and "model" African city to replace Khartoum, when the latter was burned down by the dervishes. Omdurman is still almost purely African. Its principal sights today are associated with General Gordon and the great Sudanese patriot and religious leader known as the Mahdi. One is the Mahdi's tomb.

The most remarkable mass demonstration I saw in Africa, and one of the most remarkable I have ever seen anywhere, occurred in Omdurman on February 20, 1953. More than 100,000 people gathered in the blazing open square near the mosque, to celebrate the signing of the Anglo-Egyptian accord promising independence to the Sudan. It was the largest crowd in the country's history. Leaders of rival parties spoke from the same platform, and old enemies embraced. Flags flew everywhere—the black flag of the prophet Mohammed, the black-yellow-green flag of the present Mahdi, and the red-white-black flag of the Egyptian Liberation Rally. Thousands of these flags were made by hand overnight, and were stitched together out of any kind of cloth, sometimes with the stripes going any odd way. But we saw no Union Jacks.

On the rude podium (bricks kept tumbling off of it) a spout of gas flame made a hissing illumination. Music from European violins got mixed up with music from native drums. Almost everybody wore long white gowns, and men and women both looked like ghosts suddenly and inexplicably come to life. The crowd cheered, shrieked, and chanted, as if crazed by joy. But the chief note of interest was something else. The Sudanese authorities had never had any experience of handling such a mass of people, and few police were available. Boys with staves led visitors to their places. But everybody behaved with complete correctness and discipline; the proceedings were swift and to the point, and there was no disorder or confusion of any kind.

From Khartoum we drove down to visit the Gezira and have a glimpse of Wad Medani (population 57,000), capital of the Blue Nile province. The Gezira is a narrow triangle between the White and Blue Niles, and resembles—in miniature—the "fertile crescent" of Mesopotamia. It covers 1,000,000 acres, has 26,000 tenant farmers, and is probably the best-run and most productive project of its kind in all Africa. It dates from the opening of the Sennar Dam in 1925; funds to build it came originally from the United Kingdom.

Today the scheme is a joint enterprise among the Sudanese government on behalf of the people, the tenant farmers, and the management. Forty per cent of the profits go to the Sudanese government, and this constitutes a substantial share of the country's revenue; another 40 per cent goes to the tenant farmers, and the rest to the Gezira Board, a public agency which runs the enterprise. An official handbook states that tenants here enjoy a higher standard of living and greater land security than any other farmers in Africa.

The Gezira project is, to define it in a word or two, a scheme to grow long-staple cotton and other crops by means of irrigation. Holdings are restricted to forty acres, and the tenant plants, in strict rotation, ten of these to cotton, five to grain, and two to fodder. He gets free water, and the grain and fodder remain his own. Engineers say that, more than any region in the world, the Gezira provides ideal circumstances for a development of this kind. Water flows by gravity from the Blue Nile to the White, and the slope is so gentle that no erosion problem exists. The soil is hard clay, and loss from seepage is negligible; the canals do not have to be bound by brick or tile, and are no more than simple ditches. Thus a million desolate acres have been made to burst with flower and seed.

Along one canal our car frightened a camel. The beast became hysterical and bolted; we followed it for several miles, helpless and unable to stop it. Bird life is wonderful in the Gezira. We saw thousands of demoiselle cranes, marabou storks, and other birds. If a huntsman shoots a grouse, his Arab bearers will race pell-mell to the bird to cut its throat before it is formally declared to be dead; otherwise they cannot eat it, because of a religious taboo.

The Moslem religion makes itself strongly felt in all sorts of ways. We paused for a drink of lemonade at a supervisor's house and had to wait for a while in our car, in order to give the ladies of the household time to scamper away and hide. Non-Moslems are, of course, not permitted to see unveiled Moslem women in the Sudan.

Approaching one end of the Gezira, we became totally lost. There was no trace of any kind of track. We wandered around helplessly, by car, for several hours. Our guide said laconically, "It's hard to know where to drive when you can drive anywhere." This

parched, violently dusty emptiness, obliterated by clouds of dirt, was what the whole Gezira was like before the irrigation project got under way.

The Sudan has another important reclamation and development scheme in the Zande area, nine hundred miles away near the Congo border. This too is symptomatic of the way progress is coming to much of Africa, even if it comes slowly.

Background to Today's Politics

The Sudan has a complicated history, which for many years was dominated by a bitter rivalry and struggle for power between Britain and Egypt. Now, as an independent state, it is busy making its own history, and promises to make it well.

In 1819 Mohammed Ali, a despotic Egyptian ruler, sent his armies into the Sudan and conquered it. The period of Egyptian rule which followed lasted until the 1880's, and was unimaginably cruel, slothful, and corrupt. About 1881 rose the tremendous Sudanese prophet and warrior, the Mahdi, who became famous all over the world. The word "Mahdi" means Messiah; the real name of the Mahdi was Mohammed Ahmed. He built up an army of tribesmen known as dervishes, and in the name of Allah fought a savage rebellion against the British and Egyptians both. This Mahdi was a very notable personage indeed. He claimed to be a descendant of the Prophet Mohammed. He was what we would call nowadays a fanatic nationalist with strong religious overtones. He died young, at thirty-seven, but before his death he succeeded in freeing most of the Sudan from Egyptian tyranny.

Beaten to their knees, the Egyptians in the Sudan turned to London for help. What followed is a famous tragedy. After prolonged delay and uncertainty, the British government finally sent General Charles George Gordon to safeguard British interests in Khartoum and superintend Egyptian withdrawal from the area. (Gordon has always been known as "Chinese" Gordon, because of his previous experiences in the Far East.) He was not, as is often thought, sent to Khartoum to conquer the Sudan for the British, but, on the contrary, to help evacuate it. But he was a cranky character, and he made his own policy. His forces and those of the Mahdi soon came into conflict. The Mahdi's men advanced on Khartoum, and after a prolonged siege took it in 1885. Gordon was killed by the dervishes on the steps of the Governor's palace just three days before a relief expedition arrived to save him. Controversy about all of this exists to this day, and hardly a year passes without some new book about Gordon and his fate.

Thirteen years later the British took their revenge.

In 1898 General Sir Horatio Kitchener (later Lord Kitchener of Khartoum) wiped out the dervishes once and for all at Omdurman. This was a battle in the grandest old style. The Anglo-Egyptians lost only forty-eight killed; the dervishes were slaughtered wholesale, and lost 9,700. One of Kitchener's officers was none other than the youthful Winston Churchill. It is startling to recall that Sir Winston, until recently the British prime minister, had his baptism of fire leading a cavalry charge on the banks of the Nile more than sixty years ago!

The Mahdi died—a natural death—in 1885, shortly after Gordon was killed. Kitchener had his tomb opened and sacked, and his remains thrown into the river, as if he had been a dog. The Mahdi's successor was another religious fanatic and nationalist of great force named Abdullahi, and known as the Khalifa. The word "Khalifa" means "lieutenant." He was pursued after the slaughter at Omdurman, and was caught and killed in a remote part of the Sudan in 1899. Today he is venerated as a hero.

Then in the same year, 1899, joint Anglo-Egyptian rule was set up over the Sudan, and modern Sudanese history begins. The Anglo-Egyptian government was called a condominium, and it lasted for a little over half a century. As a condominium, the Sudan had a unique status, because in theory it was ruled jointly by both Britain and Egypt. It was neither flesh nor fowl nor good red herring. It was not part of the British Commonwealth; it was not part of Egypt; yet it was not independent either.

Soon after the condominium was established the British took first place. Egypt had theoretically equal status as ruler, but the British ran the country. Kitchener was Commander in Chief and Governor General for ten long years, from 1889 to 1899, and the man who followed him held office for seventeen uninterrupted years more, until 1916. Proconsuls had long terms in those old days. The Egyptians did their best to hold on to their rights, but increasingly they had little to say. The Governor General was always British, and he ran the government with an iron hand. Then—to foreshorten a tangled story greatly—Egyptian nationalism began to become increasingly powerful in Egypt, until Egypt finally won its independence from Britain. Meantime, Sudanese nationalism was also rising. The Egyptians—now that they were independent—resented being squeezed out of power and influence in the Sudan, and in 1951 an Egyptian government annulled the condominium and proclaimed King Farouk, who was then on the Egyptian throne, as King of the Sudan. The British refused to accept this, and an angry period of tension between Britain and Egypt began. The Sudanese themselves were torn three ways. Some (a few) wanted to stick with Britain. Some wanted to incorporate themselves with Egypt, and some—the majority—wanted to strike out for themselves as an independent state.

The British regime was archaic in some respects and expensive and it was certainly imposed on the country by force in the first place, but the British did a magnificent job in their half century in the Sudan. For fifty years their administration, based on the Sudan Civil Service and recruited largely out of Sudanese themselves, gave the country law, education, justice, public order, and almost complete political tranquillity. The Sudanese were given ample opportunity for nationalist development, even during periods of crisis. There has never been a revolt in the Sudan. For this one must pay tribute to the good qualities of the Sudanese as well as to the British. After World War II only one British battalion, say eight hundred men, was stationed in the whole of the Sudan, and the Sudan Defense Force, composed mostly of native troops, never had more than thirty British officers. Think by contrast of the number of French troops—scores of thousands—the French have to keep in Algeria!

The time came in the early 1950's when the British, bowing to the spirit of the times, decided that they had to go. They could not afford—politically or otherwise—to stay any longer. After tortuous negotiations the British and Egyptian governments worked out an agreement on February 12, 1953, providing for self-government in the Sudan. This was an epochal event. The Sudanese were given the right, within three years, to choose their own future —whether to maintain themselves on an independent basis or to join Egypt. The Egyptians thought confidently that the Sudanese *would* vote to join Egypt, and indeed an influential pro-Egyptian party, fed by Egypt, existed in the Sudan. Then came a series of remarkable elections in the Sudan, and the Sudanese who wanted complete independence—freedom from Egypt as well as from Britain—progressively became stronger and finally won. So, on January 1, 1956, the Sudan became an independent state.

The most picturesque as well as venerable political personality in the Sudan today is El Sayd Sir Abdel Rahman el Mahdi Pasha, K.B.E., C.V.O. He is almost universally known by his nickname, "Sar." He was born in 1885, and is none other than a posthumous son of the great Mahdi, who fought Gordon at Khartoum. In fact he is considered by his followers to be a prophet, like his father—almost divine. On the other hand, orthodox Moslems do not subscribe to

Mahdiism, and do not accept the "fact" of the present Mahdi's alleged divinity.

The most significant thing about Sar is that he is the spiritual leader of the Umma (Independence) party. He took the lead in the 1950's in opposing Egyptian claims and ambitions; he wanted to avoid being swallowed up by Egypt, and worked strenuously for full freedom for the Sudan. In fact, he was so markedly (if politely) anti-Egyptian that he was sometimes called a British puppet—a strange thing for the son of the old Mahdi to be called.

Sudanese friends took us over to Omdurman for an interview with Sar. He is probably the richest man in the country, because his properties have convenient access to the most valuable of all Sudanese commodities—water. Sar has four wives, and we met two of his sons; one is about fifty, and is the active head of the Umma party; one is a youngster about seven, who has an English governess. All the wives are, of course, secluded into strict purdah; we did not even see any female retainers.

Sar is tall, dark, dignified, and amiable. He wears a thick, graying beard, played with lemon-yellow beads as he talked, and (as is so often the case with potentates of this type) had on a costume that became less oriental and more Western as you looked at it from top to bottom, from north to south. His dazzling white, intricately bound turban might have come out of medieval Baghdad, but his woolen socks and narrowish yellow shoes might have come from Harlem. We had tea, lemonade, and cakes with icing colored to an almost intolerable brilliance, while Sar talked through an interpreter. Present at our audience were several ministers. Then entered a celebrated Sudanese personality, Sheikh Babikar Bedri, who is ninety-six years old and who has devoted most of his life to advancing the cause of education for Sudanese women. He was barefoot, and he kissed the Mahdi's hand three times loudly, with moist smacks. This alert and humorous old man, like Winston Churchill, fought at Omdurman sixty years ago.

A WORD IN SUMMARY

It remains to pull a few loose threads together. The Belgian Congo is as interesting as any place I have ever been in the world. Belgian rule is practical, businesslike, and stern; it has done a good deal for the Africans, and before very much time has elapsed it will probably be obliged to do more, if only from the point of view of Belgium's own self-interest. Ninety-seven thousand Belgian whites will not find it easy to deny political expression and civil rights to more than twelve and a half million black Africans.

The United Nations performs a distinctly valuable service in Africa, watching over the interests of half-a-dozen Trust Territories scattered throughout the continent. One of these is Ruanda-Urundi, which is administered by Belgium. Here Pygmies and giants combine against a landscape of unexampled luxuriance and splendor to make what is one of the greatest potential holiday spots of the world. Moreover, the Albert National Park, one of the most marvelous repositories of wild game left on earth, is close by.

To the east of the Congo is Uganda, a British protectorate. Some of British Africa is still politically asleep, but not Uganda. Here, against an almost savagely colorful backdrop and amid many surviving medieval customs, a modern nationalist movement is developing, and will sooner or later have to be dealt with in mature long-range terms. Next door is Tanganyika, another UN Trust Territory which is ably administered by the British. It is not so advanced politically as Uganda, but advance will come.

To the west is French Equatorial Africa. French rule in Black Africa is more temperate, wiser, and more likely to produce a stable future than French rule in other parts of the world, like Algeria. The French policy of assimilation is working fairly well—if slowly—in Equatorial Africa, and, thanks to the foresight of General de Gaulle, most French territories below the Sahara have now achieved internal autonomy within the French framework. This is a remarkable forward step.

In French West Africa nearby political and social advance has also been precipitous, and this is true of the Cameroons as well. The Cameroons will probably attain full independence in 1960.

As to the Sudan, this great state, formerly under Anglo-Egyptian rule, has at last achieved complete national freedom. It has handled its new responsibilities wisely, and, though faced with many obstacles and difficulties, is progressing well.

Dr. Schweitzer dislikes the growth of African nationalism and probably laments much in contemporary African policy and patterns. But Schweitzer, magnificent a human being as he is, represents the past more than the future.

Equatorial Africa, like most of the rest of Africa, is on the march. Yesterday is gone. This spectacularly challenging part of the world—that of the Congo and its neighbors—is growing up fast, and its legitimate aspirations merit not only our interest but our intelligent and discerning sympathy.

INDEX